The Essential Guide to

LIVING A STRESS FREE LIFE

Personal Rejuvenation for the New Millennium

ANTHONY S. DALLMANN-JONES, Ph.D.
author of
Phoenix Flight Manual
and
Primary Domino Thinking

Graduate Professor
Teacher Education
Educational Psychology
Marian College
Fond du Lac, WI

Another fine book in the
PRIMARY DOMINO THINKING
Series
by

Wolf Creek Press

Author: Anthony S. Dallmann-Jones, Ph.D.

ISBN#: 1-881952-28-2

Wolf Creek Press
P.O. Box 463
Fond du Lac, WI 54936-0463
920/921-6991
920/921-7691 (Fax)
editor@wolfcrk.com
http://wolfcrk.com

The Essential Guide to Living a Stress-Free Life is gratefully:

Published by Wolf Creek Press, Fond du Lac, WI
Typeset by MasterProof, Eau Claire, WI
Printed by Data Reproductions, Auburn Hills, MI
Distributed by Associated Publishers Group, Nashville, TN

Dedication

To:

–

The most important symbol is the –
A tombstone has two dates separated by it.
Your life is going to be represented by that dash.

This book is dedicated to your personal journey.
It should be a lot more than a dash.

Foreword

*Just like in business,
stress does not kill you—
mismanagement does.*

Wherever I go in this magnificent world of ours and relate to people that I sometimes work in the field of stress management many roll their eyes and sigh, "Stress? Could I use you! I've got stress like you wouldn't believe!" I refrain from embarrassing people deliberately, but I probably could just by asking these same people to explicitly define *stress.* Few individuals know what stress really is . . . and yet all are hampered by it.

To be imprisoned by something and not even know what it *is,* much less know what to do with it is tragic. William Blake said it perfectly:

*"In order to escape from prison
first you must realize that you are in one!"*

I want you to be one of those individuals no longer imprisoned by such unnecessary ignorance. This book is designed to give you the knowledge you need to be street-smart about stress as well as some definitive techniques to **do** something about it. I want this book to be a very personal *I-Thou* relationship between us, and I want this material to be highly effective for you.

What does this ask of you?

1. Be *humble* enough to realize you need to learn.
2. Be *willing* to apply what you learn.
3. Be persistent until it is second nature.

What can I promise you?

1. I will give you the benefit of all of my experience in this incredible area of stress-free living from my years as a psychotherapist, a teacher of stress management courses and seminars, and my consulting with schools, businesses and Fortune 500 companies over the last 15 years.

2. I will give you straight-from-the-shoulder information that has been field-tested and *has worked* for people (many less intelligent than you) and it will be clearly stated and organized with no baloney (humor aside).

3. I will do my best to make this a fun read, but you and I must never forget that this is a serious topic. After all, stress management IS a matter of life and death.

4. I want to be here for you past the book, just as stress issues and concerns will be, so if you have questions after you read and apply what's in this book, please e-mail me your stress management questions at asdjones@iosys.net and I will personally answer them.

Now, let's get serious . . . and have fun doing it.

Anthony S. Dallmann-Jones, Ph.D.

Table of Contents

1

Stress and Choice

It is important to acknowledge that the *choices* you make in the Here & Now determine your future. If you *choose* to sit in the middle of the street and do **that** right now, you will have a different future than if you *choose* to continue reading this book. Agree?

There was a 38 year-old woman in one of my classes that wrote: "I know it sounds silly, but until now I never realized I had *choices.* I had always gotten up in the morning and did just what I had to do until I went to bed that night. I never even considered that I had a *choice* in what I might do next . . . and I'm working on my Master's degree!" A lot of us "react" to life as if we were merely one in a series of falling dominoes instead of the Primary Domino itself. [We'll talk more about *Primary Domino Thinking* later.]

A famous French moralist, probably Voltaire, once remarked that all our problems begin once we leave our room. I might amend that to read: "All our problems begin once we leave our *womb.*" The astute philosopher or psychologist, however, understands that all our problems, especially stress, really begin with an initial conscious *choice,* a deliberate decision **not** to accept things (reality **or** our experience of reality) the way they are. Then, we go on to maintain that stress through a continuous chain of *choices* to retain resistance as a strategy while still concluding that things are not okay the way they are. "I don't like it and I won't like it, nor am I going to learn from it and make different *choices* next time," states the man or woman bent on creating and/or sustaining stress.

So, you may not know at this point exactly which *choices* to make in order to alleviate a lot of your stress, but you **will.** It is sufficient right now to know that when the time comes you do, indeed, have the power to make *choices,* and those choices will route your future.

Admittedly sometimes individuals consciously or by default remain in the same patterns that are not helpful or necessarily healthy. This, in effect, is **choosing** to stay ignorant and helpless. This is not a put-down; it can be a shrewd decision to remain helpless. What **is** dangerous is being unaware of the consequences of choosing to be ignorant or helpless.

I am saying that it is crucial for you to know in your heart of hearts that you do have the power of *choice-making,* just as you chose to read this book rather than bake a cake.

Important: All humans have stress . . . except for one bunch, and we have a special name for them: *Cadavers.* Stress is synonymous with life. Stress doesn't kill you, **it is your inability to manage stress that kills you.** Even if it's only killing you slowly (on the installment plan) it surely is raining on that personal parade called *your life* (-) on a regular basis, isn't it? If you con-sider the quality of your life important, then there is good reason to pay attention here.

Most of us have not only a super-abundance of highly stressful situations to get through, but most of us were also raised by people who wouldn't know effective stress management if it bit them in the hinder parts. Further, as children our tense family "situations" often taught us inappropriate, strange, unhealthy and/or dangerous methodologies for dealing with them.

These weird, ineffective or destructive attempts at handling stress should be unlearned or surrendered as useless. Stop a moment, reflect, then write down some of the stress management techniques you learned from your family which are **not** working for you in your life today. [Let's get off to a good start here: You need a pen or pencil with you while going through this book, so get one and fill in things as I ask you to, okay? Remember that *procrastination* is one of the greatest stressors, so: Do it NOW, please.]

Non-productive/destructive stress management techniques I learned from my family:

_____

_____

_____

_____

_____

_____

_____

_____

_____

_____

_____

_____

_____

_____

_____

_____

_____

_____

Get used to writing throughout this book. It will increase effectiveness exponentially. Let this book become your personal journal as you make a conscious decision to learn and improve the quality of your life. So, keep the book. It is not a loaner. Let your friends buy their own. (Or, better still, buy a dozen and give them away!) The point is, make this book your own by interacting, writing, and reflecting in this all-important area of stress management in your life. What is worth spending time on more than you?

I might as well tell you now that effective stress management aimed at creating a wonderful life will involve some life-style changes. But we will do it gradually, gently, and not only will it be fun but you will be rewarded daily as you see things getting better and better one day at a time.

Be patient, persistent, and hang in there! I promise you that you will be able to come back and read what you have written and see just how far you have come.

Vocabulary

You and I need a common language to maintain our clarity of communication, so let's agree on some vocabulary:

Stressor: *anything, positive or negative, that urges you to make an adjustment or change from what you are currently doing.*

Note that I said *positive* or *negative*. Stressors often come in the form of good news as well as in the form of the evening news. In my city a fellow won the lottery for over $110,000,000. The stories on how profoundly this changed his life—and not always for the better—are well known around here.

Vacations, supposedly designed to relieve stress, actually provide their own unique variety of stressors. Why? Because by definition vacations ask you to make adjustments. The demand to make adjustments is the stressor. This also explains why *boredom* is a stressor, since it literally begs you to make adjustments: "Geez, do something different, will you?"

It is important to note that **stressors vary from person to person,** and this alone can cause many disagreements. The volume on my stereo was not a stressor for me but it certainly was for my Mom—even through a closed door! Those unique events or attributes that irritate (or thrill) us show up as just part of that thing we like to call *personality.* For example, "pet peeves" are individualized irritating stressors. *I* don't like the sound of silverware on teeth—*you* may have never noticed. *You* are very put off by the appearance of our property when the garage door is left open—*I* could care less. *I* never balance my checkbook—*you* are uncomfortable if you don't balance yours as soon as the monthly statement arrives.

Stress: *a reaction to a stressor.*

It is very important to remember that **your reaction to a stressor is mental/emotional/physical all at the same time every time whether you are consciously aware of it or not.** Unawareness of this fact explains how stress can sneak up on you with ulcers, cancer, heart attacks and other nasty little surprises.

Distress: *damage to the system.*

That's you. You are a system—actually a number of systems: circulatory; excretory; reproductive; digestive; neurological; muscular, skeletal, lymphatic; respiratory; immune. Any and all of these systems are affected adversely by ineffective stress management. So are your emotions. So is your mind. In this book, we will regard your mental, emotional, and social systems as not only as tangible as the physiological subsystems mentioned above, but actually the commanders of them.

In any particular individual, exactly which system will distress, how it distresses, and when it distresses is a mystery. It seems a choice made by one's nature, and will unfold automatically until someone or something *intervenes.*

Intervention: *providing different choices.*

Remember this for later, or sooner as the case may be, because stress management is all about deliberate self-intervention (making a conscious *choice* to modify or influence the current path being followed. Humankind is probably the only species capable of becoming adept at this skill.

Common Signs of Distress

When your cup runneth over with too many stressors (and how much constitutes *too many* is, again, unique to each person) *or* you have too few tools, skills or choices to handle the stressors that are appearing, you enter doors with the sign DISTRESS above them. These signs are feedback that *intervention* is called for. Ignore the signs and here are some of the price tags:

- *Physical:* headaches; ulcers and other digestive problems; hypertension; fever blisters; backaches; insomnia; certain forms of cancer; chronic fatigue.
- *Emotional:* persistent depression; persistent frustration; persistent anxiety; persistent impatience; persistent loneliness; persistent boredom (the feeling you feel when you won't/can't feel your feelings).

- *Mental:* self-rejection; loss of creativity in problem-solving and decision-making; dissociation (splitting off from yourself); insecurity; procrastination; hyper-criticalness; obsessive thoughts.
- *Behavioral:* compulsive habits; chronic interpersonal conflicts; chronic complaining; withdrawal from relationships.

Wow! How can all these maladies come from something so common as that little thing we all experience called *stress?* Let's learn a little more, then you will see clearly why and how it happens.

Never forget that *knowledge is power.* So? Well, being "stressed" is all about being powerless to handle something effectively, so the more knowledge you have the more effective you will be. Therefore, it is important for you to grasp in a big way the knowledge that follows.

The Stress Cycle

Humans are supposed to be *homeostatic,* meaning in a balanced state. This balanced state is maintained by responding to feedback in the form of sensory input from the environment. The occurrence of a stressor in your life sends you into an alarm state signifying a decision may be needed to self-correct the imbalance. The pause while one contemplates (or avoids) the decision places you in a state of *resistance*. This state of resistance is physical (muscle tension), emotional (negative feelings), and mental (a "make-wrong" declaration).

The longer you stay in a state of negative-resistance or avoid making a decision as to what to do about a particular stressor, the higher your chances for distress. Overstaying your time in resistance/negativity/indecision will lead to exhaustion or "burn-out." To make a decision to unhealthily adapt (a few of the limitless examples are smoking, drinking, workaholism, temper tantrums, overeating, etc.) will also result in exhaustion. [Exhaustion, unfortunately, makes itself so very convenient with a front as well as a back door!]

The goal is to make wise adaptations so that you can have a happy and healthy life.

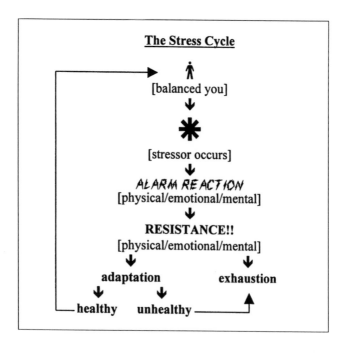

If, however:

a) Your life-teachers (parents/grandparents/ preachers/educators/caregivers) failed, out of their own ignorance or absence, to teach you appropriate healthy adaptive tools and skills; and/or,

b) at the opportune moment you were incapable of lesson absorption for some reason or another, then you are set up for "burn-out" sooner or later.

Usually it is **sooner** because life keeps making demands whether you have healthy stress management tools or not. This means that a person will more often than not utilize whatever is handy, including unhealthy, compulsive and ineffective habituated patterns of response to demands for change. Why? Because bad breath is better than no breath at all.

The rest of this book is a description of some of the most powerful tools/skills available to deal healthfully with stress.

There are five compartments in the dynamic stress management "toolbox":

- Mental Tools
- Physical Tools
- Emotional Tools
- Social Tools, and the
- S*ecret Compartment,* to be revealed later.

Remember, whenever you artificially break things into specific categories in reality there is always a "crossing over" between categories. For example, how can you truly separate "social" experiences from "physical" or "emotional" ones? I construct the book this way for you to facilitate some type of order and cohesiveness, but after you follow my advice in the next paragraph they will all blend together naturally . . . as they should. After all, stress is often not predictable, so you need to carry all your life management tools with you at all times.

My advice is to read each tool in each compartment carefully—experiment with it after reading it—then look for opportunities to use it in "real life" (there is usually no shortage of these opportunities!) and continue field-testing it until it has proven itself "under-fire." Persistent use of any tool will facilitate it becoming automatically available when needed. It takes about 30 days of practice to automatize a tool/skill.

I
MENTAL TOOLS

2

Locus of Control, Limits and Boundaries, Power

Your mind is your greatest ally and your greatest enemy. Ironic that the very part of you that can solve problems, make healthy decisions and generally assist in bettering your life, can turn on you like a junkyard dog.

There is no doubt that negative past experiences, poor habit patterns, and bad role models have determined some of your current programming that's not in your best interests. **There is not one good reason why new decisions cannot redetermine your future programming more healthfully.**

Shortcut: ACCEPTANCE

There is a very complete and compatible Eastern approach to quickly resolving a lot of stress; and it allows us to keep our opinions and attachments which we hold so dear! A good name for this method might be Delayed Begrudging Acceptance. It consists simply of stepping back a level and saying: "I may not like things the way they are, but that's okay because . . ." [You fill in the blank.] . . . because I'm going to do something about it/ . . . because I can't do anything about it/

13

. . . because there are more important things on my mind/ etc. etc. In other words, we end up accepting the greater picture, which includes our current determination not to approve of some of the particulars, as well as our many past disapprovals. Stated more positively: We choose to enjoy, embrace or love it all (the good, the bad and the ugly) including even our desire to hate some of it and our experience of feeling displeasure with some of it.

This, in a nutshell, is the intellectual version of the resolution of all stress. And it gets easier as time goes on. For stress or "negativity" to persist in our lives, we must continually:

a) insist on (choose over and over) our non-acceptance at all times on all levels; or,

b) make a conscious rejection and then "finalize" it by forgetting/suppressing it.

If ever we admit that at some level a particular stressor is okay then, while the problem may still remain, the stress associated with the problem will begin to disappear. The reason is: our problems don't create our stress. **We create our own stress** by not accepting our problems and by insisting that we find no pleasure, benefit, solace or redeeming value in them.

Your Locus of Control

Locus comes from the Latin word for **place.** In a human, *locus of control* denotes where the source of one's power is felt to be located. If you have an **internal** locus of control you see a high correlation between your choices and the outcomes in your life. If you have an **external** locus of control, you see little correlation between your choices and the outcomes in your life.

External Locus of Control.......Internal Locus of Control	
Empowerment ➡	
☹ Victim; irresponsible;	☺ Empowered; responsible;
☹ Unhealthy and dependent;	☺ Healthy;
☹ Little ability to do anything but suffer/hope or enjoy handouts.	☺ Ability to make good things occur and fully enjoy the results

Empowerment is the process of moving from an external locus of control to an internal locus of control. It denotes actualization of the potentiality of the person to self-design his/her world.

Limits and Boundaries

Make it one of your goals to realize you have an *internal locus of control,* because the truth is you really do! You establish your locus of control best by deliberately choosing to set healthy limits and boundaries. *Limits* are how far you will let yourself go. *Boundaries* are how far you will let other people go.

Examples of *limits:*

"I am going to walk two miles today."

"I will do the dishes later."

"I will refrain from using profanity."

"I will not call Bill today."

"I am going to eat 2200 calories today."

"I will rest and relax all day Sunday."

"I will obey the Scout Law."

Examples of *boundaries:*

"You can't talk to me that way."

"No, you cannot borrow $5, because you never repay me when you say you will."

"You can touch me, but not like that."

"You kids will have to fix your own lunch today."

"I won't tolerate sexual innuendoes from you."

"Please don't call me anymore."

"Please don't let your dog come into my yard."

Power

Power is an odd thing. If you believe you have it, you do, and if you believe you don't, you don't! Most people wish they had more power. But almost everyone fails to realize the truth about the source of that power, which makes the power impossible to find!

 All of your power comes from within.

You do not have to go anywhere, or to anyone, or buy anything, to have more power—you already have it! Your issue with power is not finding it, but in effectively using what you already have. In other words, it is a *delusion* (an untruth that is believed to be true) that you are powerless. Humans with an external locus of control are living a delusional existence . . . no wonder they feel so anxious! This truth does make the job of empowerment a lot easier than if you had to locate power somewhere "out there." You must, however, be willing to uncover the power you do have. What hampers you from knowing your true power?

The remaining chapters in this section will offer you some mental empowerment tools that will change your life.

3

Old Tapes

We were born small. Everyone was bigger, had more experience, and knew everything. That's the way it seemed anyway. We took it all in as if it were Gospel, which was a smart thing to do considering the size of those people!

Yep, we had all these racks of blank cassette tapes in our little heads just waiting to be filled up, and everybody sure seemed eager to do that. They probably wanted to help us out—who knows?—but they could only program us with what they had on the tapes they had in *their* little heads, right?

We believed those authority figures then, but some of those tapes are just not helping us today, and may even be limiting or destructive. So it's time to realize that: **Although up until now our past programming has determined our choices, there's no reason why new choices can't determine our future programming!**

To do this, first let's look at the tapes you have:

a) Consider the following list of the authority figures from your childhood who may have made negative tapes in your head.

b) Cross out any that do not apply to you.

c) Add any that are missing.

My personal tape-makers:

mother

father

grandparents
older siblings
relatives
peers
preachers
teachers
your culture
doctors
dentists
nurses
counselors
coaches
priests
nuns
mentors
media
heroes
babysitters
spouses
abusers
bullies
your neighborhood & neighbors

_____

_____

_____

_____

d)   Next to each active name write out the
     tape(s) that person made/recorded in your
     mind and place quotation marks around it.
     (*Breathe nice and circularly while you do
     this.*) Examples: Dad: "You'll never
     amount to anything!" Mom: "You never
     were very graceful." (Use extra paper if
     needed.)

e)   Now challenge the current validity of each
     tape **while considering the tape-maker
     as you know them today.** Ask yourself,

> *"Don't I know more **now** about myself than they did **then?**"*

f) Rewrite the tapes with the truth, as you need it written to help you recover and deal optimally with stress today. Why not be your own tape-maker?

Examples of counteracting tapes:

Negative Dad tape:
"You'll never amount to anything!"
Positive remake: "I amount to a great deal!"

Negative Mom tape:
"You never were very graceful."
Positive remake: "I'm as graceful as I care to be."

Take your time and do this thoroughly. It is well worth the effort. Don't be surprised by all the insight and emotion this process creates. Just breathe and relax and stick to it. If it takes you some time to do this, fine. But please do not go on in the book until you have completed this. I promise you that you will *never* look back and say, "Boy, was that exercise a waste of time!"

4

Recontextualizing

Life is full of things, people, and events. Some are high up on our list of favorites and some are not. This is, of course, what makes life exciting as well as frustrating. The ones that we deem low on our list of preferences do add variety, but the drawback is that not everybody or everything agrees with us like we want them to do!

Think of it as if each person has two holsters on their hips: One is filled with +'s (make-rights) and the other is filled with −'s (make-wrongs). As we experience things, people, and events, we habitually assign each of them a value. We rather righteously stick +'s and −'s on everything as if it were the absolute truth. The *real* truth is that **we can choose** to put +'s where we usually place −'s if we want to.

Exercise

Recontextualize a flat tire so that it's not a "make-wrong":

> "I wonder how fast I can change it?"
>
> "This will give me a chance to go back to sleep."
>
> "This will give me a chance to accept help."
>
> "Now I can empathize with all people in similar circumstances."
>
> "Well, it is only flat on one side!"

"Thank goodness, a chance to practice recontextualizing!"

Recontextualizing does not mean you give up your right to change something, it just means you now have a choice to either accept it the way it is or enjoy it during the process of changing it a lot more than if you were hating it.

Some think that the way to motivate yourself to change things is to kick yourself in the rear with hate. Hate creates resistance, and **resistance actually creates persistence.** What I am saying is that it is a lot easier to change something if you accept it than if you reject it. You will understand this a lot more when you get to the section on Primary Domino Thinking.

Think seriously about actively recontextualizing. It has great implications for enjoying everything a lot more . . . for seeing problems as a challenge rather than something to anticipate with dread. Just practice it for a few days until you get the hang of it, and you will see what I mean.

List some things and deliberately change their contexts such that they trouble you no more:

_____

_____

_____

_____

_____

_____

_____

_____

5

Affirmations

Affirmations are positive thoughts that can be written, read and/or spoken. Why bother? The purpose of "doing affirmations" is to replace negative, self-abusive stress-producing thoughts with positive self-enhancing ones. Since **all behaviors begin with thoughts** it appears to be a good investment to establish the roots of behavior as healthy and enjoyable.

[Note: Affirmations themselves can be utilized as a separate stress-reduction device. They are simple to do, and they do work. But if you want to crank up the power, first learn how to do affirmations well, and then incorporate them into the Primary Domino Thinking section that follows later. They form a naturally powerful alliance for you.]

Adults often carry from childhood an abundance of negative thoughts concerning self-esteem, the habit of co-dependence, personal ability to succeed, the need for abuse, etc. If trying to undo old self-limiting programming, I suggest that you generate a list of your personal negative limiting thoughts, and then, by writing the contradictory positive counteracting statement, you have created an affirmation automatically! Some additional affirmations are suggested after the guidelines that follow. Please adhere to the following section for maximum benefit.

Sample Affirmations

Following is a variety of sample affirmations that may be helpful. There are some that may fit your work situation, others that focus on your personal life, and many may overlap both. If some of these affirmations fit your personal needs, please use them, but be sure to rewrite them if necessary so they sound like you talking to you.

1. I like and respect myself. I know I am a worthy, capable, and valuable person.

2. I enjoy my life, my profession, and my relationships with other people.

3. I have pride in my performance and a positive expectancy of the future.

4. I am very effective and efficient, especially in stressful situations.

5. I guide my own destiny and I am accountable for the results of my decisions and actions.

6. I am very firm, decisive, and self-confident.

7. I have an excellent free-flowing memory with clear and easy recall.

8. I am well organized, and I vividly and explicitly know my plan of action.

9. I am fair and just in dealing with people.

10. I enjoy taking calculated risks to improve.

11. I show concern for others' feelings.

12. I develop feelings of self-respect and esteem in others.

13. I am an action person; I do first things first and one thing at a time.

Take some time to work on specific affirmations for yourself. Remember: An affirmation is simply a one-sentence definition of a quality, a characteristic, a habit, or a material goal you strongly desire to become a reality in your life.

The easiest way to write an affirmation is to select the change you want in your life, then clearly picture in your mind how you would act with the new pattern of behavior in your life. Next, write down a vivid description of your picture in one sentence, and there's your affirmation. Be sure to include your senses: how it feels, what you see, how it sounds; and put the description in your own words and style, just as you would say it so that it sounds like you.

Guidelines for Writing Affirmations

(Some of the following ideas are with permission of The Pacific Institute of Seattle, Washington, but it's been so long since I asked and they gave it and I have modified so much that I can't remember which pieces are theirs. Sorry and thanks, PI!!)

Here are some guidelines for making positive, present tense written affirmations:

1. *Personal:* You can only affirm for yourself. Do not try to affirm qualities or changes in other people to correct or alter situations you cannot control. In writing your affirmations, you are changing your "regulator" (your self-image) through personal positive statements. In most cases your affirmation should be an *I* statement.

2. *Positive:* Write out your affirmations in a positive sentence structure. Do not describe

what you are trying to move away from or eliminate.

3. *Present tense:* Write your affirmations in the present tense. The reason present tense is used in designing affirmations is that this—the present moment—is the only time frame in which the subconscious operates.

4. *Indicate achievement:* Do not indicate the ability, "I can," in your affirmation, because this will not produce change. **You already have the ability.** What you must indicate concretely is actual achievement. Begin statements with "I am" and "I have."

5. *Action words:* Describe the activity you are affirming in terms that create pictures of you performing in an easy and anxiety-free manner. Your subconscious actions should be described by statements that start with: "I easily . . ." "I quickly . . ." "I enjoy . . ." "I love to . . ." "I thrive on . . ." and "I show . . .".

6. *Emotional charging:* Try to put as much excitement in the wording of your affirmations as you can by vividly stating your behavior in colorful terms. Words that spark an emotional picture in your subconscious mind help to make the experiencing of your affirmation more believable and attractive.

7. *Accuracy:* It is important for you to affirm only as high as you can honestly imagine yourself becoming or performing at this time. The rule of thumb is to not overshoot or undershoot. Try to have a clear and

vivid picture of the end result you want to accomplish.

8. *Balance:* A vital aspect of the process is that all of your affirmations (goals) should fit together in a consistent manner. Try not to be affirming in inconsistent directions. Balance is the key. Look at growth in all areas of your life rather than just one or two.

9. *Realistic:* In writing out your affirmations, do not try to affirm perfection. **Your investment is not in perfection, but in excellence.**

10. *Keep it to yourself:* Your personal affirmations should be private. Others may constantly try to remind you of the "old self-image picture" of yourself. Without really meaning to hold you back, people around you may get upset when you start changing and growing.

Imprinting

Imprinting is the action step needed to impress your goal on the subconscious. It is simply a three-step process of reading, picturing, and feeling.

a) *Words:* Read the words of your affirmation, several times each day. There is nothing magic in reading the words other than to have a consistent trigger. The best times to read and imprint your affirmations are generally early in the morning or anytime during the day when a relaxed time is available.

b) *Pictures:* As you read your affirmation, you should be vividly picturing and experiencing yourself clearly having accomplished the change you want or the end result you intend to create. Through this experimental visualization, you are displacing old self-images with new pictures of how you want to feel and act. Remember, you are practicing and experiencing the change consciously to begin with, but through picturing you are turning your expectations over to the subconscious mind. Very quickly you will begin moving easily and naturally to your new performance reality.

c) *Feelings:* Feeling the emotion you want is important for increasing impact. Gather up the feelings based on your five senses that you know will accompany the accomplished goal. Enjoy them in vivid detail each time you imprint your affirmation. The affirmation will affect your system in a positive way in direct proportion to the frequency you use vividness and emotional involvement.

Generally speaking the imprinting of your affirmation can be broken down this way:

Just reading an affirmation:	10 % impact
Reading and picturing:	55 % impact
Reading, picturing, and feeling:	100 % impact

Imprinting through visualizing the right picture with emotion speeds the change process dramatically.

Your purpose in using affirmations is to overlay the current images in your subconscious with a predetermined outcome in the form of new images and emotions. For example, in weight loss, you are changing the "picture" regulator of how you look or how much you should weigh. Once you have programmed in the new picture, you cannot tolerate the old, and your creative subconscious helps you reach the new picture. It may be through dieting, exercise, changing habits, or some combination of actions. [A very detailed high-powered form of personal sculpting, or deliberate self-design, is found in the mother book of the PDT Series: *PRIMARY DOMINO THINKING . . . Creating the Life You Want.* See the back of this book.]

6

Interactive Affirmations

Interactive affirmations are an important form in that they actively counteract your mind's negative responses to your affirmation with another positive affirming statement (which in and of itself may lead to other affirmations). Notice that there are 3 sets of 3 in 1st, 2nd, and 3rd person. This is because we have self-negating tapes stored subconsciously in each of these ways.

Overheard conversations (3rd person) are quite powerful in our self-regard tapes. Stored authority figure tapes (such as parents, teachers, preachers, older siblings, grandparents) who addressed us directly (2nd person) have major influence upon us for most of our lives. It is crucial to counteract each of these if one is to root out all deeply stored self-abusive programming that sets us up for stress in our lives.

Sample Interactive Affirmation

Be as clear and specific as you can about what you are going to change. In the example below it involves overcoming the anxiety of sudden changes, a situation previously feared. Each of your mind's responses should be a) reflexive; b) uncensored; and, c) with no repeats. Notice you put your name in the beginning of the 2nd and 3rd person sets.

1)   I handle sudden changes easily.
     (Your mind's response)
     *(Affirmation to handle this response)

2)   I handle sudden changes easily.
     (Your mind's response)
     *(Affirmation to handle this response)

3)   I handle sudden changes easily.
     (Your mind's response)
     *(Affirmation to handle this response)

1)   Tony, you handle sudden changes easily.
     (Your mind's response)
     *(Affirmation to handle this response)

2)   Tony, you handle sudden changes easily.
     (Your mind's response)
     *(Affirmation to handle this response)

3)   Tony, you handle sudden changes easily.
     (Your mind's response)
     *(Affirmation to handle this response)

1)   Tony handles sudden changes easily.
     (Your mind's response)
     *(Affirmation to handle this response)

2)   Tony handles sudden changes easily.
     (Your mind's response)
     *(Affirmation to handle this response)

3)   Tony handles sudden changes easily.
     (Your mind's response)
     *(Affirmation to handle this response)

I handle sudden changes easily.

Sample of the Sample

1) I handle sudden changes easily.
    B.S.!
    *It is absolutely true that I easily handle changes!

2) I handle sudden changes easily.
    I get weak when sudden things happen.
    *I gain strength from sudden changes.

3) I handle sudden changes easily.
    My mouth gets dry when something sudden happens.
    *My mouth is as moist as it needs to be.

1) Tony, you handle sudden changes easily.
    You fall apart!
    *I face sudden changes calmly.

2) Tony, you handle sudden changes easily.
    You hate sudden changes!
    *I love everything about sudden changes.

3) Tony, you handle sudden changes easily.
    You are afraid you can't handle changes.
    *I am eager to face sudden change.

1) Tony handles sudden changes easily.
    Tony comes unglued.
    *I laugh in the face of sudden change!

2) Tony handles sudden changes easily.
    Tony is incapable of handling the tension.
    *I can handle anything easily.

3) Tony handles sudden changes easily.
    Tony is too rigid.
    *I am very capable and flexible.

I handle sudden changes easily.

Note: The last sentence in each set is always in the first person. This is because you are effectively counteracting and reprogramming what your mind says about what you and others say about you. [Read that again.]

Interactive affirmations are effective if done 10 times a day for one week. Asterisked responses may lead one to deeper negative tapes that are more important than the original one. These sometimes pop up into your awareness and can become new potential affirmations to be done interactively with the same formula.

Affirmations can also be taped and played back, made subliminal and, of course, plastered all over your home, car and office. It is important to be consistent and persistent in doing affirmations. They **do** work and they work quite well.

7

Primary Domino Thinking*

Primary Domino Thinking is a most powerful tool for self-actualization. It is so powerful, that I have seen it succeed even for people who have never enjoyed success with anything. It is, therefore, the most potent and far-reaching intellectual tool for effectively preventing distress known at this time.

---

* NOTE: Although a relatively simple process once internalized, this *Primary Domino Thinking* chapter is a large one! As your coach, I want to offer you two options—choose one that appeals to you:

1. Work right through the chapter, interacting and internalizing as you go so that you experience and learn the material now.
2. If your time is limited, just *read* the chapter and return later to do the applications. Don't skip the chapter because much of the chapter material that supports the tool, *Primary Domino Thinking*, is highly useful in and of itself.
3. Non-option: Do not skip the chapter, as it includes some understandings that you will need in later chapters.

But while we are "noting":
NOTE: Despite the length of this chapter, what you are getting here is a very abbreviated form of a powerful tool. If this little bit grabs you, I strongly suggest you obtain the source book in this series: *PRIMARY DOMINO THINKING ~ Creating the Life You Want ~* from your local bookstore, library, or with the convenient order form in the back of the book.

Primary Domino Thinking is simple to understand, easy to use, and costs nothing—one merely
needs knowledge of *Primary Domino Thinking*
and a conscious mind for it to work. Sound like
magic? It is . . . the natural magic you were born
with taken to the ultimate realization of your
potential.

The process of using *Primary Domino
Thinking* moves you in the direction of supreme
self-reliance. It uncovers potential powers inside
you that you never knew existed. It maximizes
those powers as a ruby crystal does when trans-
forming an ordinary beam of light into a powerful
laser ray. *Primary Domino Thinking* can be quietly
utilized anytime, anywhere, enhancing not only
you, but everything and everyone around you!

Your thinking creates your world—my thinking creates my world. Your thinking changes your
world or keeps it the same. My thinking changes
my world or keeps it the same.

Primary Domino Thinking is a tool. It is a 5-
step process designed to create self-determined
improvements in your life. The transformations
may be long-term, such as changing your finances,
relationships, career, or body. Transformations can
be more short-term, such as changing your present
mood, attitude or outlook. The transformations
could even be athletic or recreational, such as
improving your golf or bowling score, batting
average, or swimming skills.

It makes no difference what type of improve-
ment is desired, the steps are the same. In order to
utilize *Primary Domino Thinking* one basically
needs nothing more than knowledge of the 5-Steps
and what you came into life with: Consciousness
and Breath.

The 5 Steps of *Primary Domino Thinking*

Step 1: Passionate Possession
To have impact, you must dare to get close.

Step 2: Exploration of the Problem or Issue
Investigate the problem, discovering the true owner.

Step 3: Composing the Primary Domino Thought
Generate your secret formula.

Step 4: Primary Domino Thought Implantation
Tip the Primary Domino!

Step 5: Regulation
Monitoring and adjusting makes the difference.

Each step will now be briefly described. At the end of each section there will be space for you to work through a chosen issue of your own, step by step as we go along. I heartily encourage you to take the time to do this.

"If you cannot apply what you have learned, nothing has been learned."
—John Dewey

How Primary Domino Thinking Works

First, let's think backwards. Let's take an ordinary event in a person's life as if we had filmed it, and were viewing it in slow motion and in reverse order:

4. Any **outcome** in your life is a result of your behaviors. (e.g., I wound up at the restaurant and had a good time.)

3. There were **behaviors** that led to the outcome. (e.g., I dressed, pulled the car out of the garage and drove here, met my friends, ordered my food and had some conversation and laughs with my friends, thereby winding up at the restaurant and having a good time.)

2. The behaviors that led to the outcome were a result of your **thinking.** (e.g., What should I wear? Red blouse? No. Too bright for the restaurant. Blue, maybe? Yes. Etc.etc.etc.etc.etc.etc.etc. Open the garage door. Back out carefully. Good. Etc.etc.etc. Turn right. Etc.etc. Turn left. Etc.etc.etc. Shall I meter park or use the parking garage? Hmmm, it could be a long lunch and I don't want to have to run out and plug the meter—I might miss out on some great conversation—so I will use the parking garage. Turn left. Get a ticket. Which ramp? Etc.etc.etc.)

1. At the head of all those thoughts was a *Primary Domino Thought* that started everything falling into place. It is the most powerful thought in the bunch because once it was firmly *implanted* everything else happened almost automatically. (e.g., Hey, I think I will give Janet, Rosie and Jenni a call and see if they want to have some lunch. That would be fun!)

All human change begins with a primary thought. To take this a step further, actually *all* outcomes are determined by *Primary Domino*

Thoughts. The reason for the *PRIMARY DOMINO THINKING* book is to show you how to design a *Primary Domino Thought* that will create the outcomes you desire deliberately. The proper formation of the *Primary Domino Thought* and the effectiveness of its implantation always determine the outcomes in your life.

Primary Domino Thinking Can Be Negative

Pieces of your life not good for you can be locked into place by repetitive negative *Primary Domino Thoughts.* And if you are experiencing chaos in your life it can always be traced back to subdued and/or random *Primary Domino Thoughts* that are created by chance, old tapes, habits, and/or lack of deliberation.

If your life keeps turning out like crap, then find the destructive Primary Domino Thoughts buried at the bottom of the pile. They are always there. When you find them you will understand everything about the sewage in your life.

—Me

Again, the purpose of this section of the book is to turn this around for you. Rather than being confused by life or "victimized" by your old patterns you can learn to deliberately implant positive or remove negative *Primary Domino Thoughts* that will transform your life automatically for the better.

The usual way we bring about change in our lives is to focus on the struggle with plans, behavior modification, rewards, punishments and guilt. What we focus on expands. We focus on the struggle and struggle we get. *Primary Domino Thinking* has proven that the reason we succeed so infrequently is that we do not know the secrets of true personal transformation. It is much easier than we have believed, if we but know the method.

PDT focuses on a) correct identification of the problem; and, b) development of the magical *Primary Domino Thought* that, once released, will take care of our problem for us. The *Primary Domino Thought* causes all the changes to happen automatically without any conscious effort, struggle, or even planning. We just need to put in our five minutes a day with PDT, then go about our lives basically "following our nose" and listening to the directions that come from within.

Primary Domino Thinking Step 1: Passionate Possession

Most people's number one strategy for dealing with stress is to run like hell. It's a natural response, you know. Probably our soft-bodied species survived so well because it could run faster than those with a hard carapace. And this is all well and good if you are facing physical danger: Run, run, run away and live to play another day.

BUT, most of our stress is hardly physical endangerment. It's more like *frustration, anxiety,* and *tension* which, interestingly enough, our mind today reacts to as if we truly were in danger of being severely damaged or even dying. Running away from mental issues is not as easy *if* it's even possible. Why? Because we carry them with us! Physical dangers are outside of us, but frustration, anxiety and tension are inside jobs! Running from these makes us look like cartoon characters running from our shadows.

Stop this! We must start doing exactly the opposite. Start taking ownership by taking 100% responsibility for your stressors right now whether or not you believe it will work.

Responsibility

Most people don't like the word *responsibility* because as children we never heard it said with a smile. Responsibility was always toned as burdensome or laborious. Our poor ancestors carried around that false puritanical thinking, and even felt they were handing us a gift with the attitude: "Suffer big loads of responsibility and someday you will be rewarded." Maybe that half-truth worked well enough to keep them going, but not without a lot of wear and tear, as you have probably observed. The part of the half-truth that is true is that responsibility *is* good; the part of the half-truth that is **not** true is that responsibility should be a burden.

 Responsibility is the key to liberation.

One is obviously powerless to change things peacefully without being responsible for them in the first place. If I don't want to be on the Buildings and Grounds Committee, then I forfeit my opportunity to decide where the new shrubbery will be placed. If I want to be able to do something about my anger, then it is in my best interest to *own* my anger. If I am uncomfortable with my child's behavior, it is smart to mentally acknowledge my part in co-creating the situation.

Responsibility is an *investment.* To take responsibility for everything that happens in your life is an investment in *you*. Taking responsibility *does not* mean we are unable to hold others accountable for their behaviors. It *does* mean we definitely hold ourselves accountable for what we do with our life here and now, i.e if somebody drops a hot potato in your lap, your first "response-ability" should be to take care of yourself. If, for example, you suffer an injury caused by another person's carelessness, it is in your best interests to concentrate on what you are going to do with yourself now, rather than concentrating on self-pity or repetitive fantasies of retaliation.

At any moment in time you are either responsible for yourself or you are a victim—it is always your choice.

—Me

Again, you have no control over modifying that for which you are not responsible. Having no responsibility over a situation is akin to being a victim in that particular situation. This book is mostly concerned with your internal state from which all things flow (or don't flow) for you. When speaking of responsibility know that it begins *within,* even if the observable results of responsible behavior are seen *without.*

Responsibility begins with *thought.* So, let's have a new thinking about responsibility. No matter who or what you have been blaming for your condition, your problems, your emotions, your whatever up until now, rest assured that it is in your best interest to believe the following from now on:

I love everything about being responsible for everything I experience—or refrain from experiencing!

It is important to memorize this statement and think it to yourself 20 times a day no matter how much you currently dispute it. After a few days (or less if you are a fast learner), when you see the truth and power of this thought, you will have a wonderful experience of empowerment. You won't need to repeat it anymore because you will **know** it to be true.

If after a few days you still have trouble accepting it by just thinking about it, write it out ten times a day. When you "get it" you will smile or laugh.

Just this realization about responsibility alone is worth a fortune. Without this realization, I assure you that very few vital wonderful things are going to happen by your design in life.

Primary Domino Thinking Step 2: Exploration of the Problem

Problems that are correctly assessed do not remain problems for very long. If a problem hangs around for awhile, it's a good bet that it has been inaccurately assessed.

This is usually true because a correctly stated problem has a built-in solution and you, being fairly smart, would have immediately taken steps to solve the problem as you have always done, e.g., "I'm hungry because it has been five hours since I have eaten food." Solution: Eat some food.

For many of my clients, once the problem was clarified our work together was finished, and they went off confidently to do what they knew clearly had to be done. Much of my work as an educator and psychotherapist has been that of a problem-clarifier rather than a problem-solver. Most of us know what to do if we just clearly know what it is that needs to have something done about it!

Foggy Stressors

1. Misidentifying the Owner of the Problem

People often identify stressors correctly, but misidentify the true owner of the problem, e.g., "It drives me nuts when your room is a mess . . . what's wrong with you!" It makes you feel and even appear less than sane when you are trying to own and solve somebody else's stressor . . . and this is a **very common** dilemma.

A client of mine had a female friend with compulsive behaviors that he kept trying to fix by pointing out her problems, giving her articles to read, arguing with her, manipulating situations, and even speaking with professionals on her behalf. Her compulsions worsened. His response was to redouble his efforts. This strategy created even more compulsive energy until the woman was eventually spending over eight hours a day in her behavior. He had misidentified his problem as her behavior, which left him with no recourse but to continue his unsuccessful efforts at controlling her. Against both their desires the relationship, due to overwhelming frustration, wound up as an abusive one.

At issue was: To whom does the problem behavior belong? The answer was apparent: her behavior was her issue and hers alone. His problem was ignorance in knowing how to productively associate with a loved one burdened by compulsive behaviors. Once this realization became internalized by each of them, they were free to concentrate their energies on solutions that would really work.

2. Ignorance & Stubbornness

Major internal blocks to solving problems often boil down to some combination of *ignorance* and/or *stubbornness*. Either a person doesn't have enough knowledge about the problem and/or its solution (ignorance), or when the needed knowledge is obtained, the person is unyielding in an old pattern and refuses to apply what could work (stubbornness).

Many humans are more concerned with being *right* about not changing destructive patterns than being healthy and happy. Strange as it may seem, people often choose to die rather than change.

How many people actually die of "terminal righteousness" just because they are too stubborn to change their unhealthy ways of thinking?

Ignorance in a particular situation means a lack of internal tools and skills (information and processes) to modify that situation. It is in your best interests to have enough *humility* (knowing your current limits) and *willingness* (motivation) to continually expand your knowledge base. Stressors present the opportunity and motivation to do just this (providing a good reason for you to be grateful for the next stressor that you are fortunate enough to have come your way!). Each problem solved expands your holdings and your chances for success in the next problem arena, and so on and so on, exponentially.

In other words, sometimes it behooves you to *learn,* in the classic sense, about a problem by reading, asking, pondering, researching, digging, and absorbing. Not to worry: If you don't have the necessary motivation to seek out new information, Step 4 will often create that drive in you, sometimes seemingly out of nowhere.

The assessment phase is where precision begins to play a critical role in effective stress management. If the key area of concern cannot be accurately pinpointed, you are left with an ineffective strategy akin to shooting at noises in the dark or, worse still, shooting at the wrong target in the light.

These strategies of random-shooting and wrong-targeting are, of course, the most often used approaches to problem-solving. This explains why many problems are never satisfactorily solved.

3. Wrong-targeting

It is interestingly tragic how people can be so snappy with solutions that do not work and how slow they can be to realize this. Sadly, many proposed "solutions" are actually just poor attempts at explanation. These poor explanations become futile attempts to solve a dilemma. For example,

a) "I don't feel good about my finances, but I just can't stop spending."

b) "I can't find peace because my neighbors drive me crazy."

c) "My interest in spirituality is lagging—churches are filled with only pseudo-Christians these days."

Notice how externally located the implied solutions are in those explanations:

a) Spending controls how I feel.

b) The neighbors are in charge of how peaceful I can feel.

c) Others are in charge of my spiritual development.

If you locate potential cures for your problems "out there" the results will be zero. Problems are usually not "out there" and, if they were, the solution would probably be obvious.

 Problems are located within.

Believing anything other than this is almost always wrong-targeting. Disowning a stressor leaves one powerless to do anything reasonable and workable about it. It is no wonder people acting to solve their problems on the basis of constant misdiagnosis begin to feel, and even appear, nutty. As a good graphic representation of this, imagine what would happen if you dropped a brick on your foot but for some reason located the pain in your right ear. There you are hobbling around looking for ear treatment, trying to convince everyone (and yourself) that there really *is* a problem with your ear. Can you relate this to anything in your life?

_____

_____

_____

_____

_____

_____

_____

_____

_____

_____

4. Dishonesty

The origin of a stressor is often clouded by lack of honesty. Real integrity is rare. Lack of integrity—or inaccurate or incomplete disclosure—exists because of fear-filled childhood experiences of being punished for being honest. Fear of honesty is based upon a belief that "If the truth becomes known, I will suffer in some way." By the time humans have reached adulthood they have seen ample proof of this, and have evolved elaborate schemes to fool others—and themselves.

It is unfortunate that children often get punished for just being kids. All child abuse and neglect is perceived by children as a message that says "You are not good enough the way you are." A child's fear and/or willingness to please is their first sacrifice of integrity: "I shall pretend to *be* (think/feel/do) someone I am not." Children are reinforced in this strategy by the subsequent withdrawal of the punishment or even by being rewarded with a smile, a goody, or a loving touch, thus imbedding the strategy of sacrificing integrity for the sake of relieving pain or gaining reward. It worked then—it may have even been seen as the only way to survive—and it still works just well enough for adults treating each other and themselves like children to reinforce itself. **But nothing works as well as honesty!**

Now that you are an adult you can lay aside
deceptive childhood strategies for surviving and
being loved, and you will be safe.

Oh, you may get a few raised eyebrows
because you suddenly get honest, since people will
probably notice a definite change in you. But I
haven't heard of anyone being killed by a raised
eyebrow since back in '06!

We must exhibit here in Step 2 the same willingness that we utilized in Step 1 to passionately
possess the problem. Now we must answer the
question: "Honestly, just what is the real problem
here?" Refuse to accept your own snappy answers.
If you instantly feel you have the answer to an
ongoing problem, that's probably *not* the answer.
Be willing to get even more honest—and more
honest still.

*Be honest: Maybe you don't really want a solu-
tion!*

One can only begin to wonder if there isn't a
hidden investment in *non-solution* in some cases.
For example, parents who continually find things
to criticize in their children may have a need to
have power over something they can control. So, it
really won't matter how much the kids improve,
there will be no end to the criticism. The *source* of
the tirades may be the real problem and not the
child's spotlighted behavior.

Consider people who continually *worry* over
things but never do anything about it except worry
some more even when a way out is offered. Maybe
they don't really want a solution to this stressor.
Perhaps there is a pay-off in non-solution, such as

getting attention, or feeding a really bad habit of *self-pitying.*

Self-pity is one of the most destructive practices to a self-actualizing life known to humankind!

Self-pity is often at the root of most addictions, compulsive behaviors, and violence.

5. Lack of Focus

Sounds redundant to say that you can have lack of clarity about a stressor due to lack of focus, but here I am talking about a deliberate strategy of nonfocussing. Reliable identification mandates a willingness to focus on the problem . . . to be *with* the problem . . . to *get close* enough to the problem to notice how it ticks. This means rejecting avoidance strategies such as ignoring, daydreaming, fantasizing, medicating with the ingestion of food/alcohol/nicotine/drugs/etc., changing the subject, quick dispensation, "ozoning," "problem-hopping," or compulsive habits.

Wow, coach, if you're going to take away all those customary and comfortable patterns of avoidance, what's left?

Instead, sit quietly with an assessment mentality while doing Conscious Connected Breathing and you will eventually know what you need to know. Have faith in the ability of this simple strategy. It is easy and effective.

I keep talking about this Conscious Connected Breathing, don't I? Go to page 135 and read up on it, practice it, and then come back here, OK?

What if the problem really isn't yours?

Back in Step 1 you assumed possession of a problem passionately in order to get close enough to determine not only clearly what the problem was, but also *true ownership* of the problem. Upon further investigation in Step 2 it may be discovered that you actually do *not* own the problem formerly possessed in Step 1. If this is true, a solution known as "giving it back" could now be instituted.

Giving Back Problems That Don't Belong to You

Giving it back is a proactive mindset that provides significant mental relief and liberates you to get on with important things in your life that you *can* do something about.

Giving it back is the security of, once and for all, knowing that an issue is truly no longer your problem. This allows you to lift the burden from your shoulders and to walk away free of the necessity of finding a solution.

Giving it back is primarily a conscious internal decision, but you can also formally and verbally give it back. This means engaging the person and informing them that:

"This issue about _____ is not MY problem—it could be YOURS. I am personally through with it."

Use these words pretty much verbatim in person, via mail, or telephone.

If they do not accept the problem, that is not your problem either! But if you have to live or work with that person, then you may experience the challenge of learning to live with someone that has a problem and denies/avoids it. If you let their ineptitude at problem ownership bother you, then THIS becomes your problem, but this is much, much easier to handle than attempting to solve a problem that wasn't yours in the first place!

Attempting to solve someone else's problem is as futile as trying to convince your mother that you are indeed now grown up.

Primary Domino Thinking Step 3: Composing the Primary Domino Thought

The previous steps were dedicated to clearing away the fog around these two important criteria for success. Step 1 of *Primary Domino Thinking* instructed on the how-to of passionate possession. Step 2 helped you get a grip on the exact identity of the problem.

If it has been determined that the problem is not "mine," then the problem has, by now, been surrendered to the proper authorities, right? But if the problem has found its home in you, and you have gained some decent clarity on its makeup, then you are ready for Step 3.

Formulation

Step 3 is also known as the *formulation phase* of *Primary Domino Thinking*. Don't let that scare you with its technological ring. It just means that in Step 3 you are going to convert the problem explanation you derived in Step 2 into the actual *Primary Domino Thought*.

At this point I want to offer some notes of encouragement: I understand we all look for short fast answers that promise immediate and permanent relief. But be honest: How many fulfill the promise? Few, if any.

I also understand that *Primary Domino Thinking* may look a little tedious, but it won't for long. Once you internalize the process, it will go more quickly every time you utilize it. And you will carry the tools to transform your life with you from now on!

The Mind

One of the brain's passengers is a little engine, best known as the *mind*. The mind makes a great slave, but not always so great a master. Step 3 concerns putting the subconscious part of the mind to work as the laborer for which it was intended. Step 3 makes the mind exponentially effective at carrying out our plans.

The mind has many capabilities, but those capabilities are best served by a certain type of very specific instruction. *Primary Domino Thinking* is a very specific way of getting maximum performance from your mind-engine. Learn it well, and the mind will deliver unto you what you want, as a good paid employee should.

Converting a Stressor into the Primary Domino Thought

Once a stressor has been clarified in Step 2, a simple but essential conversion is called for in Step 3. The conversion is similar to the preparation of food for assimilation into the body—that process called *digestion,* a series of food transformations starting with chewing and swallowing.

Again, the conversion from a Step 2 explanation of the problem to the development of a Step 3 *Primary Domino Thought* is known as *formulation.* This consists of rephrasing the explanation into a proactive *positive solution* statement, just like you did in the previous section on *affirmations.* If, for example, you think "It curbs my appetite" is the reason for overindulging in sweets, then a potential *PDT* might be "I am as full as I healthfully need to be."

To further get the flavor of this, some examples will help clarify this part of Step 3. The *Primary Domino Thought (PDT)* in each example listed below is italicized beneath each stressor.

Stressor: I get angry when ignored and I feel unimportant.
PDT: *I am always important.*

Stressor: I don't feel good because I am overweight.
PDT: *I have a sleek physique.*

Stressor: I hate this work because my job is boring.
PDT: *This work excites me.*

Stressor: I am uncomfortable because my lower back is tense.
PDT: *My back is relaxed and loose.*

Stressor: Thoughts of mom irritate me. She is always critical.
PDT: *My mother cares about me.*

Yes, you are correct, your initial gut-level reaction to a *Primary Domino Thought* might be

"Ridiculous!" or "B.S.!" or "How stupid!" If that is the reaction you get then you are probably on the right track. Let me assure you that most *Primary Domino Thoughts* will only be so disdained by you for a short while—**until they come true!**

The way you test a potential *PDT* is by assessing whether or not if it came true the stressor would disappear. If it would, then you know you have arrived at an appropriate *PDT.* If not, then restructure it so that it does.

Understand that the whole purpose of *Primary Domino Thinking* **is to make the** *Primary Domino Thought* **become absolutely real in your life.**

You can see, therefore, how important it is to take the time necessary to arrive at a great *PDT.*

Guidelines for Great Primary Domino Thoughts

We usually try to make changes in our life by using the inefficient trial and error method. Because of the inefficiency of trial and error methodology there is a reasonable guarantee of large amounts of wearing and tearing, not to mention terribly poor odds of success. So most people just give up and settle for what they already have. This is why there is so little change in people's lives despite their pain. It also explains how most of us become so adept at just "living with it" as our major form of expertise in life adjustment skills.

It is very, very smart to narrow the number of error trials as much as possible by utilizing your intelligence to select and sharpen the most appropriate *PDT.*

Primary Domino Thoughts are high-powered *affirmations,* a positive mirror image of the stressor. Their purpose is to replace a negative, self-abusive, stress-producing, disempowering thought with a positive, self-enhancing, empowering one. Since all behaviors begin with thoughts it appears to be a good investment to make sure the roots of a behavior are healthy and enjoyable.

How do you determine if your *PDT* is a good one? Remember these guidelines from the section on affirmations to help you test them.

- **Personal:** You can only modify yourself.
- **Positive:** Use only positive language.
- **Present tense:** State PDTs in the present tense.
- **Indicate achievement:** Begin statements with "I am . . . ," "I have . . . ," "I do . . ."
- **Action words:** Describe the activity you are modifying in terms that create pictures of you performing in an easy and anxiety-free manner.
- **Emotion words:** State your behavior in vivid terms.
- **Accuracy:** It is important for you to modify only as high as you can honestly imagine yourself becoming or performing.
- **Privacy:** Your modifications are personal and should be for you only.

Creativity in brevity is also encouraged in order to maximize impact. One reason why those sentence-length mental affirmations that were at one time popular were not very effective was because the string of words was too long for the subconscious mind to digest.

Have Fun

The best way to learn how to create *Primary Domino Thoughts* is to continue to play with them. Let yourself be creative and have some fun. When you have created an effective *Primary Domino Thought* you can easily tell by another "Aha!" reaction you will feel inside. The *PDTs* you need will easily click in automatically once you get the hang of it.

Primary Domino Thinking Step 4: Implantation

All previous steps and their explanations and preparations were important, because they bring us to this moment of truth about permanently changing a stressor: *Implantation.* This is where the rubber meets the road—the critical point of contact that will make all the deliberate differences you desire to make. Developing competence with Step 4 will put you in the commander's seat of converting your stressors into solutions.

Because Step 4 is the most critical of the steps, as well as the most challenging, it is important to carefully define the essential vocabulary. Please take your time and internalize the following terms and their meanings before moving to actual implementation. You don't have to memorize them, just understand them. This will maximize your benefits and minimize the number of trials it takes to achieve your goals.

Step 4 Glossary

Visualization: *focusing on an internal image that is meaningful to you*

There is no right or wrong way to visualize. *Primary Domino Thinking* depends on your natural ability to deliberately and symbolically represent situations internally. Some of your *PDT* colleagues have utilized pictures (snapshots), words or their acronyms (like a typewriter/word processor in action), cartoons, caricatures, symbols, abstractions of color and movement, or film clips (animation).

Whatever form of visualization is utilized, it is *the* means of conveying a message to your subconscious system, which then actually carries out the transformation desired by automatically setting up the rest of the "dominoes" (thoughts, behaviors and events) needed to create the *outcome*—the last domino in the chain—you desire.

Do you see the difference here? The reason most people are unsuccessful at manifesting the reality they want is because they have everything bass ackwards. When they encounter an issue or problem they make up their minds in a split second as to a solution, grab onto a strategy they have used before (that probably didn't work very well then either!), and frustratingly attempt to arm-wrestle a solution all the way through to the end result they think *should* be the outcome.

Instead, our dedication is in designing and setting up the correct *Primary Domino Thought* and then sitting back and watching desired outcomes happen automatically—dynamic dominoes working for you while you sleep, go about your daily affairs, enjoy the beach, or walk in the woods!

Thought: *awareness in the here and now; thoughts are also tools for shaping (or refraining from shaping) experience*

A *thought* is in the present moment. When you boil it down, there is no awareness outside of *thoughts.* Within *thought* resides your consciousness, your experience, and all of your power. Your deliberate power is represented by conscious choice-making: *Primary Domino Thoughts.*

The way your life works (or doesn't) rests upon individual *thoughts.* This is wonderful, because a *thought* is the one thing you can totally control.* It is this realization, plus the design of the *thought* and the manner in which you implement it, that makes all the difference in successful managing of your life.

Implant: *an inserted Primary Domino Thought*

An *implant* is the deliberate insertion of a well-defined *Primary Domino Thought* into your subconscious mind. It is similar to planting seeds in the soil, i.e., *mental farming.*

Extraction: *removal of a previously instituted implant*

---

* Premium mental health is synonymous with the ability to think clearly. The more 'distressed' a person is, the less control they have of their thinking. Being out of control of our thinking is very painful because of the intense amount of fear involved. Many think a mentally ill person is in so much pain that they cannot think straight when, in actuality, the reverse is true: The mentally ill are in pain because they cannot think straight. Bizarre behavior, which often accompanies mental illness, is a twisted attempt to deal with the psychic pain, closely resembling a migraine of the soul.

An *extraction* is the removal of a debilitating thought that is no longer desired, by visualizing its representation (picture, phrase, symbol, etc.) as being withdrawn. *Extraction* is the term utilized when one is removing an old *Primary Domino Thought,* i.e., *pulling weeds.*

Extractions are done primarily when one discovers old detrimental "head tapes" that have been driving one into destructive modes of behavior. Sometimes these are negative childhood *implants* placed in us by careless or ignorant authority figures, malevolent abusers, or institutions such as schools, religions, hospitals, the media, etc.

Emotion-sensation: *concentration of energy around an emotion with the accompanying physical sensation*

Any single human experience has three doors into it. Each experience you have is obviously recorded mentally, no matter how trivial or even unnoticed it may be, but each experience also has **emotional** evaluation and physical **sensation** components. We have a tendency to separate them out, but in actuality they are merely *perspectives* of the same experience. We separate our experience into three pieces—*physical, mental, emotional*—for reasons of convenience or from habit, but all pieces are present regardless of our cognizance of them.

MOST IMPORTANT! Primary Domino Thoughts are only to be implanted when one is in a moment of feeling "good." **The following cannot be overemphasized!**

Most humans, if they think at all to self-intervene on their stress, only do so when they are feeling badly. This is equivalent to casting seeds onto a flat rock and expecting them to grow. Your chances of success rise immeasurably if you plant the seeds in rich soil where they can take root, correct? The *Primary Domino Thought* is exactly like a seed, and it needs to be implanted at a moment when one feels uplifted and the mental soil is rich.

The challenge here is that most humans don't even think to deliberately influence their own lives when they are feeling good. This is often the major differentiation between beginners and those experienced with *Primary Domino Thinking*. Rookies see the "good moment" as an opportunity to indulge as long as the ride lasts (which they feel won't be long); but when they get more experience the "feeling good moment" is seen as not only a chance to gain control over the duration of the moment, but also an opening in which to *implant* and/or reinforce a number of *Primary Domino Thoughts* to insure a bountiful future crop of positive healthy outcomes. The feeling-good-moment provides flat out opportunism with the highest of intentions and the ultimate of harvests.

Four Ways to Create the "Good Moment"

You do not have to wait for a "good moment." You can create it. The idea of creating a "good moment" is closely aligned with the ultimate goal of *Primary Domino Thinking*. In other words, if you are feeling poorly, and in that moment have a desire to do some deliberate stress reduction, the fertile ground can be created in several ways. Here are four that are particularly effective at creating.

1. Conscious Connected Breathing (CCB)

You can create the good moment by performing Conscious Connected Breathing and relaxation until you feel uplifted, and *then* the *Primary Domino Thought* can be implanted!

CCB creates a window or space in which you take control of the situation (this helps right away), inhale large amounts of fresh air (this helps), eliminate a lot of waste product through the exhale (this helps), send a message to the autonomic nervous system that everything is OK (this really helps!), and induce elimination of the source of most pain, which is ultimately your resistance (this helps a whole way big bunch!), and then: the relaxation signifies a readiness to make a shift. This is all within your control no matter what is going on in the outside world! It just takes *willingness* to do it.

2. Shifting Contexts

Another method of creating "good moments" is by deliberately shifting contexts. We know how to do this, but we rarely do it regularly and deliberately. A *context* is the way in which we regard something. I can choose to see a flat tire many ways: a painful experience; a race to see how fast I can change the tire; a challenge to find and use the owner's manual; a chance to use my AAA dues; an opportunity to meet a passing motorist; a good story for later on; etc. In and of themselves each of these contexts is equally valid. It is totally up to me how I wish to experience this flat tire. Oh, and I can also choose to react the same way I always do by staying angry at the inconvenience (after all, this tactic works so well!).

The point is, if I'm feeling badly, it has a lot to do with how I am choosing to view my situation, and I can change how I feel by changing how I consciously or unconsciously regard the situation.

Shifting contexts is concerned with making a deliberate choice to see some thing or event in a positive way as opposed to a negative way. To deliberately choose to shift any thing, person or event into a "make right" context is liberating. At the moment you decide to make it right you are at the helm of Command Central—you are liberated from any negative influence it holds over you and you become, therefore, *empowered.*

Practice brings this home. Fill in the blanks in these exercises.

Event: Flat tire on the open highway
Negative Contexts: Inconvenience; late; expensive; stuck; desperate; alone; dangerous; frightening; confused; frustrated; _____; _____; _____.

Positive Contexts: Finally use my AAA benefits; meet new people; challenge; learn new skills; good story for later; exhibit my independence; feel my dependence; _____; _____; _____.

Event: No money in my account
Negative Contexts: Broke; starve; embarrassing; stupid; not again!; no-good; bad luck; frustrated; _____; _____; _____.

Positive Contexts: Humility; better understanding of poverty; not overdrawn; money goes *and* comes again; focus on what I bought; stay home and meditate; _____; _____; _____.

Event: Terminal cancer diagnosis
Negative Contexts: Death; pain; fear; unknown; medical tests; drain on my family; expensive; _____; _____; _____.
Positive Contexts: Live for the moment; openness to love and support; spiritual development; make peace with things and people; learning experience; finally overcome fear of dying; make new acquaintances; ultimate challenge; _____; _____; _____.

Now, for practice, you do a few:

Event:
Negative Contexts:
Positive Contexts:

Event:
Negative Contexts:
Positive Contexts:

Event:
Negative Contexts:
Positive Contexts:

Shifting contexts profoundly alters your view of things, the way you feel in your body, and your predominant emotions. This means it profoundly changes your life in the moment—*exactly the right time to implant a Primary Domino Thought.*

I could not talk about shifting contexts without including a section on this topic from the master of recontextualization, Jim Leonard!*

---

* The following section is modified from *THE SKILL OF HAPPINESS—Creating Daily Ecstasy with Vivation.* Thank you, Jim Leonard!

*The Top 10 Ways to Shift Anything to a
Positive Context*

1. **Notice that what you are experiencing is
    not infinitely bad. Be grateful that it is
    this good!**

    In other words, you can always be glad it's
    not worse. This one works for me 100% of
    the time. No matter how bad anything is,
    I'm always glad it's not worse.

2. **Compare it only to itself.**

    Things can only be bad, wrong or unpleas-
    ant when compared to an imaginary stan-
    dard of how it should be. Anything is OK
    compared only to itself.

3. **Cultivate a sense of fascination with
    it—notice that it's at least interesting.**

    Anything is interesting if you just think
    about it in the right way.

4. **Expand your compassion for all people
    who experience similar things.**

    I really like what this one does for people.
    Because of what you are experiencing,
    you are uniquely capable of having com-
    passion for other people who experience
    similar things.

5. **Be open to it making a contribution to
    you.**

    Even if you can't see any benefit to it just
    yet, know that there will be benefits to it
    that you can't even imagine yet. If you
    expand your openness to getting benefit,
    you'll get the benefit that much sooner
    and you'll feel better right away.

6. **Turn the whole experience over to God.**
    This one is obviously not for everyone—
    your ability to use it depends on whether
    you believe in a God you can trust.

7. **Acknowledge that whether it's good or
    bad, pleasant or unpleasant, is purely
    up to the context you choose for it.**
    Obviously this is the truth. When you are
    making something wrong, your mind is
    going to tell you that the badness of it is
    inherent. If you simply acknowledge that
    its goodness or badness is up to you, it
    will integrate.

8. **Imagine what it would be like for it to
    be exactly the way it is but for you to
    feel happy about it.**
    Imagining this will set up a neurological
    pattern that supports acceptance.

9. **Notice the extent to which you already
    do feel OK about it.**
    I doubt that you feel *infinitely* bad about
    anything.

10. **You know you'll make peace with it
    eventually so you might as well make
    peace with it now.**
    You won't stay in a place of eternal make-
    wrong with anything. Might as well inte-
    grate it all now.

3. Humor

Another method of inducing a "feeling good"
moment is through direct application of humor.
Remember, you don't have to feel good to laugh—
you can laugh in order to feel good. Some clients
keep humorous books around to pull out and read

on specific occasions when a shift is needed. You can also visualize other things that make you smile, such as cute clumsy puppies, a Charlie Chaplin sequence, or any humorous event in your history. [See Chapter 11 on Humor for more info.]

4. Pleasant Memories

When you are not having a good moment but you want to create one, do this: Sit with your eyes closed and vividly remember a pleasant moment in your life. Picture the scenery, yourself in it, and remember all the details including the emotions that went with it. Do some CCB along with this for two minutes and notice what happens! Try it right now.

Once the good (fertile) moment is present, or created, move on with Step 4 of *Primary Domino Thinking*.

Visualize implantation (or extraction, if relevant) of the *Primary Domino Thought*.

While relaxing the body and performing Conscious Connected Breathing, *implant* the *Primary Domino Thought*. Do this by first visualizing the *Primary Domino Thought*. If one is replacing a former thought, then the old thinking must be visualized as being extracted before the new thinking is implanted.

It is of critical importance to *visualize* the *Primary Domino Thought* being inserted with a tool such as a chisel, shovel, trowel, syringe, etc. or entering your body with each inhale. In the beginning one should probably do this with the eyes closed and in a relaxed state.

Generating the Emotion of Accomplishment

Along with the breathing, relaxing, and visual-izing, effectiveness is dramatically increased by *activating* (bringing up from within) the emotional counterparts that would accompany the actual realization of the solution to your stressor—better known as the *Primary Domino Thought*. In other words, how would you *feel* if the *PDT* suddenly came true?

Generating emotion is a very powerful entry into the subconscious mind. It involves avenues of communication monitored by the subconscious and/or autonomic nervous system. This bypasses the conscious system that has often been responsi-ble for keeping you locked into the thoughts which have created the need for this re-engineering ses-sion in the first place!

Some examples of generated emotion would be:

- the emotion of elation upon feeling a sud-den burst of energy;
- the joyous self-confidence of solving a problem;
- the serenity of an alleviated headache; or
- the warm feeling of being the desired weight.

These actualizations of emotion-sensation should be done in tandem with the visualized *implantation* of the *Primary Domino Thought*. In other words, they should all be done at the same time.

Generating the Physical Sensations of Accomplishment

Imagine the physical sensations that would go with successful accomplishment as if the *Primary Domino Thought* had already come true. Place yourself inside the *visualization.* Posture your body accordingly. If vitality is your goal, then at the time of *implantation* let your body get erect, head up, eyes bright and eager while breathing fully in an energized fashion. As an example, if becoming serene is the goal, then imagine how your body would feel at watching a Pacific sunset. Can you feel the lightness, the relaxation in your tissues, the calmness in your body? See yourself as serene— feel the emotions that go with it. Get into it!

IMPORTANT: Practice

The three parts of Step 4 should be performed daily for a minimum of 5 continuous minutes for chronic stressors you are going to do serious battle with. Modify *PDTs* as you learn of more effective forms, until they are absorbed naturally into your experience. There they can be savored and enjoyed. It cannot be overemphasized how valuable patience, persistence and a sense of adventure can be in the successful implementation of Step 4.

So-called "slack periods" will now disappear for you. During the day while waiting in line, in an office for an appointment, at a railroad crossing, under the hair dryer, during commercials, at the car wash, on the subway, at the airport, on tele-phone-hold, etc., take advantage and fill these moments with Conscious Connected Breathing and implantation of a *Primary Domino Thought.* These now become great moments of productivity rather than being viewed as a waste of time.

Remember anytime you feel "good" to take advantage and quickly implant one or more *Primary Domino Thoughts*—these are valuable tillable moments when the soil is just right for the eventual harvesting of a rich crop.

Primary Domino Thinking Step 5: Regulation

The 5th Step is not always necessary, but if needed it is invaluable. The more experience you have with *Primary Domino Thinking* the less you will need this step because you will have your life right where you want it most of the time. This may be sooner than you imagine.

For now, know that *if you fail to get the results you want, then the 5th Step is critical* to refining your application of the process until you are totally satisfied. Continue to repeat and refine Steps 1—4 until you acquire precision and effectiveness with *Primary Domino Thinking* as the ultimate stress management tool.

Step 5 completes the essential loop of feedback and refinement between goals and outcomes. It provides a space to reflect upon what you hoped would happen and what actually did happen. As previously mentioned, you are strongly encouraged to "journal your journey" with *Primary Domino Thinking*—especially with:

The Step 5 Regulation Checklist

a)   What was the change desired?

b)   What *Primary Domino Thought* was utilized?

c) Was *implantation* carried out with *visualization?*

d) Was *implantation* carried out with the emotion of accomplishment?

e) Was *implantation* carried out with the physical sensations of accomplishment?

f) What unforeseen benefits occurred outside my purpose?

g) What unforeseen challenge occurred outside my purpose?

h) Were there additional areas or objectives uncovered during the process?

i) Were my results satisfactory?

j) If not, should a–e be modified and in what manner?

k) Do the 5-steps again.

Short-term stress relief is simple with *Primary Domino Thinking*, but it is indeed possible for a single application of a *Primary Domino Thought* to create even long-term results you desire. Excellent results in just one application frequently happen, and there is absolutely no good reason why they shouldn't happen every time. There are plenty of not-so-good reasons, however, and in these cases it will take a persistent and patient effort at repeating and refining the *modifier* and the derived *Primary Domino Thought* until success is achieved. You will learn from these adjustments. You will learn how to be efficient and effective in applying *Primary Domino Thinking*.

Be willing to take action again and again, if necessary. **Never give up.**

A Note About Results

That *Primary Domino Thinking* works is irrefutable because there are so many success stories, but exactly *how* the results exhibit themselves is variable, not only from person to person, but from application to application within a person. It is good advice to **let go** of the need to arm-wrestle the results from the process and concentrate on refining the process itself. The process works, but not always in the way your ego-self thinks it should. [See forthcoming chapter on the *Terrorism of Expectations.*]

 Ride easy in the saddle with controlling results; just persistently do your best and leave the rest.

8

Creating Your Personalized Primary Domino Thoughts

Q: I wonder why I am putting this in here!
A: Because I know you will truly read & heed the following disclaimer, correct?

Disclaimer: The following is not meant to replace the previous chapter on *Primary Domino Thinking! PDT* is the most powerful form of self-induced brain surgery ever invented, BUT, let's face it: sometimes you're on the move, the clock is chasing you, and you don't/won't/can't find the time to sit for five minutes and implant your *PDT* properly. I would rather you used this abbreviated form than nothing. This format will probably not be as effective as the full-blown version but it will get you through, until you can create your five minutes of implantation time.

Remember, what you focus on expands. If you focus on *hurry* you get hurry, if you focus on *lack* you get lack, and if you focus on *worry*—well, you get the picture. The purpose of creating your own personalized PDT is to give you something to focus on during your day that will open up your life, give you **more** zest, serenity, health, wealth, or whatever.

There are tons of slogans around. Feel free to borrow one, use it as is, or personalize it. Here are a few with their meanings:

For Rough Times—Making It Through

 "One day at a time."

(I don't know how to fix the past or handle the future, but I can handle today, so that's what I am going to focus on.) If times are really tough change it to *"Five minutes at a time!"*

 "Shit happens."

(Hey, every now and then, things just fall apart; don't get overly excited about it.)

 "This, too, shall pass."

(I can endure this. Nothing lasts forever.)

For Good Times—Staying on a Roll

 "Life is good!"

(Life is good.)

"Make hay while the sun shines."

(Take advantage of a good moment and plant some *Primary Domino Thoughts!*)

"Tremendous!" (in response to "How are you?")

(Life is good!)

For Rolling Your Own—Building a Bank Account

Take some time and think up some pet PDTs to carry with you. It is best if you follow the guidelines on making affirmations: Make them

- Personal
- Positive
- Present tense
- Indicate achievement
- Action words
- Emotionally charged
- Accurate (specific)
- Balanced
- Realistic
- Private (keep them to yourself)

But, heck, guidelines are there to be modified anyway, so knock yourself out with something that just "feels right," makes you giggle, or pumps you up automatically when you think about it. This should get you through until you can find your 5 minutes to do it right.

[This marks the official end of the *Primary Domino Thinking* section, but notice how nicely this next section ties in! Each of these mindsets could be a *Primary Domino Thought* in and of itself.]

9

Mindsets for Reducing Stress

Every person has to a large degree the ability to control his or her actions consciously. You can set your mind on a particular approach to life. In fact, every day we make conscious and unconscious choices. By becoming aware of our choices, we can work to ensure that they serve to relax us and reduce the amount of our stress, rather than work against us, as our choices can often do.

The twelve mental sets that follow can be used as guidelines to improve your lifestyle. Practice particularly with the ones that "grab you" and gradually weave them into your life. They can quickly become a positive part of your life. Hang with them long enough and they will be you.

1. There is no outside emotional stress; there is only my subjective response to a situation, which I control.

2. I do one thing at a time.

3. I do the best I can about a situation, and then I don't worry about it. ("I do my best and leave the rest.")

4. I express my feelings honestly to other people.

5. I think and live positively, committing myself to the highest I can be; even from "bad" experiences I learn lessons of growth.

6. I treat **all** others, especially children, with the respect I wish for myself.

7. If I or my mate (friend, colleague, business partner, etc.) are dissatisfied with our relationship, I take steps to improve it.

8. I always look for the good in all things.

9. I am aware of my own needs, rather than those inspired by competition.

10. I am not closed in; there are always options.

11. By keeping in touch with my body and its needs, I choose to be well and happy.

12. I live in the Golden Moment.

With these twelve mental sets we can, to a large degree, create our own world, realizing that a loving person lives in a loving world; a hostile person lives in a hostile world. (Take your pick.)

10

The Terrorism of Expectations

The only reason
I am upset is because
I had the audacity to think
I should know what happens next.
      —Anthony S. Dallmann-Jones, Ph.D.

There is no doubt in my mind that we each actually create our own reality or, at the very least, are *co-creative.* * How else can you explain two people facing the same experience and having two different perceptions, reactions, and even after-effects from that experience?

---

* What this means is that we may be partners in creating our reality as we live it. A second big question then arises: Co-creator with *whom* or *what?* Well, it is up to you to answer that, and answer it you should if you are to have solidarity in life. This is what we call **the** *spiritual* question. Particular *religions* **tell** you what/who the answer is. *Spirituality* begins where religion leaves off and defines your very personal relationship with a deeply held conviction of with whom/what you are co-creating. Some answers besides God and the usual deities that might fascinate you: I co-create with *my past programming (habits), other people, forces of nature, spirits, intuition, my horoscope, money, luck, etc.* What is important is for you to come up with your own answer. The chapter on the secret compartment will help with this if you need it.

Expectations are *very* audacious on our part. **Expectations are evaluations**—whether conscious or unconscious—that a person forms of oneself, another person, an event, and/or experience which lead the evaluator to then assume that the evaluation (often made on a whim) is valid. A person doing *expecting* then anticipates that the experience will turn out consistent with the evaluation-expectations, and *then acts and feels accordingly.* Since most of us are fairly poor predictors of what will happen next, it is indeed audacious, if not silly, to assume we can accurately forecast the future. Of course, that never stops us from trying!

Expectations of the Self

There could be a book written on this very topic, perhaps even a 3 or 4 volume set! But, I promised a quick read which will work, so hold onto your socks or whatever is covering your feet right now.

What has expectations of the self got to do with stress? Well, let me ask you a question: *If you were totally confident that everything you thought, said or did was as perfect as it could be, would you have any stress?* Not much, right? So, a lot of your internal stress derives from you "not measuring up" to your own expectations. It will help to understand from whence these beat-yourself-up expectations originate.

You were born perfect. Trust me on this. That's why we call the newborn a *pristine self.* All babies are born perfect, and fully programmed to accept without hesitation all the nurturing and cherishing offered. There is only one message they fully thrive on, and that is the caretakers' behaviors that say, "Child, you are just wonderful the way you are." Babies are not equipped to handle in a productive fashion anything short of that. We come into life prepared to feed off physical and emotional affirmation with only two questions about ourselves: 1) Who am I?; and, 2) How do I do it?

Most of us rely on our immediate caregivers (usually our parents) to not only give us the unconditional love and nurturing but to answer these questions by merely reflecting back to us what we are. **We are not equipped to handle anything short of this.** So, when we are neglected, punished, abused, or told warped things about ourselves, *we go haywire.* We come up with zany reactions, some of which turn into life-long strategies for handling the pain of rejection.

We have strategies that become part of our identity and, then, expectations for ourselves. There's a ton of them: whining, meanness, depression, self-pity, fear of failure syndrome (always quit before you succeed), numbness, fantasizing, compulsions, trancing-out, rebellion, conformity, and on and on ad infinitum. These defense mechanisms get solidified like *armor* into our personalities. And they are not us no matter how much they feel like it! **We forget who we truly are.**

We develop what Freud called the *ego ideal* (how we *should* be if we were *perfect*) and then run around measuring ourselves against it and constantly coming up short. Of course, this ego ideal is usually a weird blueprint made up of a hodgepodge of fun-house mirror feedback from people who rejected us as we were—already perfect—setting up a standard that was for someone else (perhaps themselves) but definitely outside our range at the time. This is why, according to psychologists, that **as adults 85%–90% of our "self-talk" inner dialogue is negative!** We are constantly berating ourselves to measure up! (See section on *Old Tapes.*)

Human Development of the "Self"

Pristine Self
↓
Who Am I? & How Do I Do It?
↓
Characteristics Highlighted by Significant Others
↓
Self-Concept Formed
↓
Characteristics Evaluated by Significant Others
↓
+'s and –'s of Characteristics Internalized
↓
Identity Formed
↓ ↑
Ego-Ideal Established
↓
Low ← Self-Esteem Crystallized → High
↓
Low ← Self-Confidence Crystallized → High
↓
Low ← Success Potential Crystallized → High

Due to culture, family issues, parental unfinished business, personal preferences, etc., only certain of our characteristics as children are highlighted by our significant others. Those chosen for evaluation are quickly labeled within the typical "good" and "bad" categories to various degrees from "Naughty, naughty, Honey." all the way up (or down) to "You'll burn in hell forever for that one, Buster!".

I was in a supermarket just the other day as a woman discovered an acquaintance with her newborn lying in a cart. She rushes up with the appropriate oohs and ahhs, a couple of cursory questions about when the child was born, etc., then looks at the baby and says to the Mom, "Is he a good baby?" The mother responds, "Ooh, yes, he's a *good* baby." I'm thinking to myself, "How bad can a 7-day old be?"

But I am glad I saw this happening during the course of writing this very chapter. It makes my point so clearly about just how early—before we even can know it's going on—we get these crazy labels stuck on us. Crazy though they may be, these labels are very very powerful in running our lives, and determining our stress and our success.

Once this identity and ego-ideal are formed they feed off one another establishing not only a stress-producing inner dialogue, but also a flight plan for one's self-esteem, which determines one's confidence which then determines one's success opportunities.

This, in a nutshell, is the whole story of how you came to be, and why you have the trajectory in life that you have. Please remember that we condensed three volumes into three pages, but in essence this is it, dear one. With just a little reflection you can see the truth of where your self-expectations were adopted from (at first without your permission) and how they continue to be like a stick applied (self-induced stress) to some part of your mind-body when you fail to "measure up." **THIS is why we are often our own worst enemy.**

If you are relating to this, you **must** turn it around to your advantage by restoring yourself to your rightful identity. You see, there is no such thing as "high self-esteem"—there is only the self-esteem you were born with: *healthy* self-esteem. And you have never lost it, you have just had it covered up with a lot of other people's judgements that have: a) accepted as truth; and, b) reinforced through trying to live down to it all these years.

Without getting all bent out of shape about it, just think of it as misguided people trying to help you and, at the very least, giving you a set of training wheels to get this far. But, like the leg braces on Forrest Gump, you don't need them anymore, and now you have the time and resources (but do you have the *willingness?*) to start *recovering* by *uncovering* the real you and celebrating that pristine self that has been hidden all these years.

No more beating yourself up with those bogus expectations, OK?

While it's fresh on your mind, write some insights about yourself derived from this section:

_____

_____

_____

_____

_____

_____

_____

_____

_____

_____

_____

_____

_____

_____

_____

_____

_____

_____

Expectations of Others

I am tempted to get so short and sweet on this section that it would sound trite, but it really isn't. Let's try it. About expectations of others: *Don't have any!*

Let me back that up a little—again shortening a volume down to a few paragraphs. As you are beginning to see, one of the job descriptions of a 21st Century *personal coach* is to research and develop transformational vehicles and condense all the material and processes down to the essentials, along with some Q&D explanations.

Eight Reasons Why You Shouldn't Have Expectations of Others

1. You don't have the right to do so because expectations are like handcuffs and, after all, this is the land of the free and the home of the brave.

2. You can't trust people to live up to expectations anyway, because they are too busy with their own agendas just like you are.

3. Don't you have enough to do without parenting someone else?

4. You set yourself up for a lot (**a lot!**) of disappointment.

5. It takes all the fun & surprise out of what people might do next.

6. People will hate you for putting more pressure on them than they already have.

7. You aren't a fortune teller.

8. You have much better things to do with your valuable energy and time—like

focusing on *your* mission (that you will soon develop).

It puts a whole new sparkle on life when you just have no assumptions about what people might do next, and don't even care. You can afford to feel this way when you realize that your mission in life is dependent only upon your own crystal clear sense of direction and personal efforts, i.e., you don't *need* anyone else. Now, is that a liberating feeling or what? You have not only just cut loose everyone else you are going to meet from now on, including old acquaintances, but yourself as well. Nice.

While this is fresh on your mind, write down some ways you shackle other people to yourself with *expectations,* thus possibly hindering both of you:

_____

_____

_____

_____

_____

_____

_____

_____

_____

_____

_____

_____

_____

_____

_____

_____

[Note: When I talk about letting go of expectations of others: I am *not* talking about letting people out of "contractual arrangements." When you hire someone for services, or if you are in a relationship where you have invested your heart (of which you only have *one,* as far as I know) then responsibility to live up to that contract is reasonably expected. This is called *accountability* and is an important part of any social or work contract. What does create undue stress is *assuming* others have committed to a contract with you when they consciously have not. Big difference.]

Expectations of Experiences

Experiences can never be contractually insured (darn it!), though all the deities know we try! Experiences pop up out of a mysterious Pez dispenser, where one is lemon-lime and the next is lemon-lime, and then, lo, what-the-heck, here's a tutti fruitti! A lot of what I pointed out about expectations of other people applies here, doesn't it? Again, you set yourself up for a lot of disappointments, you take the surprise out of life, and you basically handcuff yourself, by trying to "hold life hostage" to your set of expectations.

Q: You know what the BIG reason is for not having expectations of experiences?
A: It is silly and unnecessary.

Why is it silly to hold the feet of life experiences to the fire of expectations? Because it is like trying to push a chain uphill. It just doesn't work! Oh, I know a lot of us grew up thinking that our expectations sort of forced life to deliver what we wanted or needed, but that isn't the way it works. **Delivery comes without the expectations.**

Don't believe your personal coach? Naughty, naughty! So, let's find out: Set a personal goal that, after you stop reading here and next sally forth into life, you will do so with absolutely NO expectations of what *should* happen, *must* happen, or even *could* happen, and then watch what *does* happen. I will ruin the surprise: You will handle whatever flavor pops up just fine and will have more fun doing so. See why it's silly and unnecessary?

To take it a step further, and really **prove** to yourself that your ego-self is not in charge of what is going on in your experiences, try this: The next time you would normally do something that you normally do, such as brush your teeth or ask someone, "What's for dinner?" just refuse to do it and then see what happens. Again, I will ruin the surprise for you: *It will just happen!* You will find yourself suddenly brushing your teeth, or the answer as to what is for dinner will "appear" to you anyway. This is a very *Twilight Zone* experience in and of itself, so be prepared to have your universe shaken up! But now you will **know** why it is silly and unnecessary to think that your expectations are critical to the unfolding of your life.

Note: If you have read this book sequentially and applied as we went along you will understand what I am about to say to you: **You cannot deliberately manifest life by *expectation*, but only by *implantation*.** So, either do it right and utilize *Primary Domino Thinking* as it should be used, **OR** just mentally sit back and enjoy the parade of life without any expectations.

A True Story

Just to really make this point! As I was writing this chapter on the road while conducting a New England book tour for *Primary Domino Thinking*, my beautiful, intelligent, meticulous travel arranger and wife, Amy, had booked us into a wonderful Atlantic beachside bed & breakfast in Gloucester, Massachusetts. We arrived in the dark around 7:30 p.m., exhausted after driving all day from a signing in New Hampshire, looking forward to a three day mini-vacation on the gorgeous coast of New England. Amy had her heart set on this particular bed & breakfast as it was a place she had vacationed fondly with her parents when she was 15— so this was the highlight of the trip for her.

We rang the bell on the porch of this lovely Victorian with our baggage in hand. A lady finally answered the door with a look of surprise, then dismay, on her face when we told her our name. "I was afraid this was going to happen," she exclaimed, then informed us that she had given our room away 45 minutes ago because she thought we were not going to show up (despite our reserving with a credit card!). My wife was extremely crushed by the news. But it got worse.

The woman gently continued, "And I don't know how to tell you this, but all of the motels in the area are full." Now, **I** was crushed!

"What do you suggest we do?" I asked trying to keep an even voice.

"Well," she says, there is a young couple who are working on their home to convert part of it into a B&B. They aren't listed in the guides but they have taken overflows before in an emergency. It's a nice place. I'll give them a call, then I'll have to drive you over because you'll never find it in the dark." [She was right about that!]

As we are following the woman's car through the darkened, twisting, unmarked streets of Gloucester, Amy is inconsolable. We haven't eaten, we're disappointed, tired, and have no idea where we are going to be spending the next three days or with whom. We were fairly silent except for one of my "good husband" attempts at cheering things up—probably a waste of breath at a time like this. Although I strongly believe that "things work out" one must also fully feel one's feelings that are legitimate at the time—and we had no shortage of those. But that's part of the *human experience,* isn't it?

It turns out that the couple is at a local restaurant (the only one in that area that was open), and the woman ahead of us has located them by calling on a cellular phone, so takes us there, turning us over with a quick good-bye to these people (whom we do not know) in a parking lot. We are invited to join this delightful party going on in celebration of one couple's anniversary in the group, then proceed to have a delicious dinner of lobster and clams with some of the best mashed potatoes known to humankind!

"You'll have to follow us to the house," they informed us, "as you will never find it from here in the dark." [They were right about that!] We followed them through more dark and twisty streets to a privately gated neighborhood, which at the next day's sunrise we discovered was on the beautiful East Point with a view of the lighthouse!

As we are walking through the spacious 6000 square foot home and up the stairs to our room we cannot help but notice the numerous gold and platinum record albums hanging on the walls. We unpack our bags in a large room with a wonderful woodburning fireplace.

Well, to shorten the story: We spent three nights and two delightful days as guests of David Brown and Jessica Flynn at their B&B. David is the former lead guitarist of 11 years with Billy Joel and was a performer with Simon & Garfunkel, Paul McCartney, Julian Lennon, and others. He now has a recording studio in the basement of his B&B, and is self-producing solo albums of some of the most beautiful guitar music (of which I am grateful to have a copy) I have ever heard.

I am only upset because
I have the audacity to think
I should know what happens next.

11

Humor

Let's kick this chapter off with an appropriate story:

One day a fisherman was lying on a beautiful beach, with his fishing pole propped up in the sand and his solitary line cast out into the sparkling blue surf. He was enjoying the warmth of the afternoon sun and the prospect of catching a fish.

About that time, a businessman came walking down the beach, trying to relieve some of the stress of his workday. He noticed the fisherman sitting on the beach and decided to find out why this fisherman was fishing instead of working harder to make a living for himself and his family.

"You aren't going to catch many fish that way," said the businessman to the fisherman, "you should be working rather than lying on the beach!"

The fisherman looked up at the businessman, smiled and replied, "And what will my reward be?"

"Well, you can get bigger nets and catch more fish!" was the businessman's answer.

"And then what will my reward be?" asked the fisherman, still smiling.

The businessman replied, "You will make money and you'll be able to buy a boat, which will then result in larger catches of fish!"

"And then what will my reward be?" asked the fisherman again.

The businessman was beginning to get a little irritated with the fisherman's questions. "You can buy a bigger boat, and hire some people to work for you!" he said.

"And then what will my reward be?" repeated the fisherman.

The businessman was getting angry. "Don't you understand? You can build up a fleet of fishing boats, sail all over the world, and let all your employees catch fish for you!"

Once again the fisherman asked, "And then what will my reward be?"

The businessman was red with rage and shouted at the fisherman, "Don't you understand that you can become so rich that you will never have to work for your living again! You can spend all the rest of your days sitting on this beach, fishing, and looking at the sunset. You won't have a care in the world!"

The fisherman, still smiling, looked up and said, "And what do you think I'm doing right now?"

Humor Takes Us Away

I have a comedy channel with my cable television subscription. I enjoy the ingenuity of some of the comedians and the laughs, too, but I also enjoy the candid shots of the audience as they get lost in watching the comedian do his/her *shtick*. The carefree look of eagerness and anticipation on all those adult faces is just so *sweet*. For a while they have forgotten their cares and the assumed need to have broad shoulders and are just swept away in having a good time.

Their faces have that bright-eyed shiny youthful look, just like my boys did when they were little and I would first see them bouncing around in their cribs in the morning. Yes, their diapers were full, but they forgot all that when they saw me and knew I would take them away from the confines of their beds into a bountiful, exciting, limitless new day full of experience. **This** is the metaphor for humor.

Humor Is Surprise

If you think about "jokes"—only one form of humor—then you will see in them the element of surprise clearly. An example:

A fellow walks into a pub and orders a beer from the bartender. There is only one other guy sitting at the far end of the bar, and he slides down next to the new fellow and says,

"Hey, I couldn't help noticing your accent, friend, where ya from?"

The fellow looks at him and responds, "Ireland, born and raised."

"Hey!" the guy exclaims, "Me, too! Let's drink a beer to Ireland."

So they do.

The first fellow looks over and says, "What part of the dear country, were you born to?"

"Dublin, my friend, the greatest city in the world!"

"Me, too!" the first guy whoops, "let's drink another to dear old Dublin."

So they do.

A little later the second guy asks, "So, where did ya graduate, if ya did?"

"Course I graduated," the second guy counters, "from me dear alma mater, St. Mary's!"

"Well, I'll be!" says the second guy, "me, too! Let's drink another to dear ol' St. Mary's."

So they do.

"So," says the first guy, "What year did ya leave the hallowed halls of grand ol' St. Mary's?"

"1962," replies the second guy.

"Well, unbelievable!" says the first guy wiping a tear from his eye, "me, too! Imagine that! We must have another beer to the greatest class ever graduated from dear ol' St. Mary's, the class of '62!"

So, they do.

About this time another guy comes into the bar sits down and orders a beer.

"Well, what's going on?" he says to the bartender.

"Not much," the bartender replies nodding in the two fellows' direction, "except the O'Malley twins appear to be tying one on again."

It is easy to see the element of surprise at work here. If I had started the joke saying, "One of the O'Malley twins walks into a bar where the other one sits . . ." there's no humor!

Humor Breaks the Ordinary

Life without humor, like people without humor, is tedious and routine to say the least. Humor is a great *temporary* stress reliever because it "takes you away" from the *tedious* and *routine,* two soul-deadening stressors.

I do want to reemphasize the serious point that humor is usually to be regarded as a temporary aid, and not a cure, for ongoing stress. For example, as illustrated so well in the sitcom *M.A.S.H.,* humor in the midst of the insanity of war and the intense stress of performing surgery under combat conditions helped alleviate the pressure of the moment, *but it did not stop the war.*

Humor May Aid in Denial

Humor can even be used destructively, as a means of denying that what one *really* needs to do is make a change and to stop merely joking around about it. *But,* if that is all you have available to you until you can come up with a more proactive strategy, then know this:

 You don't have to feel good in order to laugh. You can laugh in order to feel good.

This is why I strongly suggest to people to own some joke books, or "fun readers." If *Calvin & Hobbes* compilations lift your spirits, or *1001 Stupid Slogans & Bumper Stickers* gives you a giggle, then have them around.

Humor as Therapy

Many have heard of Norman Cousins therapeutic work with humor, started when he himself overcame a paralyzing and painful disease of the connective tissues—supposedly incurable. Norman rented dozens of comedic films and watched them every day until he was ill no more. His self-experiment not only caused his illness to go into remission, but helped create a very helpful and prolific modern health field known as *psychoneuroimmunology,* studying the relationship of mind-body interactions upon personal health. In his book, *Head First—The Biology of Hope,* Cousins states:

"In view of what is now known about the role of endorphins [released by the brain during laughter] not only as a painkiller but as a stimulant to the immune system, the biological value of laughter takes on scientific validity." [Cousins, pg. 145]

Today we know that the brain is the source of a major apothecary to the rest of the body, and laughter writes the prescription for many naturally self-produced miracle drugs that offer hope and healing.

Humor as Romance

Not only is humor about surprise, but so is surprise the better part of romance. This is why—a big secret revealed here, fellows—appropriate humor is one major requirement in successful pick-up lines! This is also why cards and flowers for no reason are more special than flowers and cards on special occasions. If you want to keep your intimate relationships special, care enough to pleasantly surprise.

A major point to be made here is that humor is not just jokes and one-liners, but can be a way of *romancing life. Romance* (different from "passion") is light-hearted and always has a bit of *anticipation, delight,* and/or other corollaries of *surprise.* I think the person who invented Post-It Notes should have gotten some kind of award. What a wonderful way to romance someone and/or lighten their day by slipping little messages unexpectedly onto people's mirrors, work stations, pillows, or in their suitcase, brief case, or lunch box.

Humor can be a friendly way of saying I *care about you* enough to take the time and energy to plan a way to put a smile on your face without warning. That is very romantic.

Humor Can Be Risky

I have been known to have the annoying habit of seeing humor in things that others are taking *very* seriously. There is something quite humorous to me when a group of Ph.D.'s, meeting as an *ad hoc* college faculty Wellness Committee, spend hours debating about how expensive a future flower arrangement for a colleague's potentially dead aunt should be in comparison with a potentially dead grandmother, or a potentially dead spouse. My humorous take on the matter was incorrectly seen as unappreciative of people's arduous efforts (not true, not true, I still defensively maintain!). But I bet you see the humor in turning, what should be a natural outpouring of compassion, into a *Sliding Scale Sympathy Index,* don't you?

The risk in humor is because the very nature of *surprise* postulates that one cannot know the outcome. Some of the funniest things I have said were not funny in other places with other people—but I took the risk because *it's worth it.* If no one is willing to take the risk in lightening up someone else's day, our whole social world is going to turn into concrete. Dare to be funny, light-hearted, romantic, and surprising.

 It is better to be outrageous than outraged.

Because humor originates as something mental that then bridges into *feelings,* what could be better than this chapter as a segue into the confusing, mysterious, and sometimes scary world of emotions and stress?

II
EMOTIONAL
TOOLS

12

What Are/Aren't Emotions?

Emotions are your instant psychosomatic (mind-body) evaluations of stressors. Some of these are universally agreed upon, such as the reaction to an object landing in your eye, or someone yelling at you (except in a New York deli where you expect it). Others are learned and are not so universal, such as your reaction to certain foods or someone staring at you.

Most of us believe that there is little we can do about our emotional reactions, meaning they seem to be a "truth that cannot be changed." Indeed, they do **feel** that irreversible because they have become *automatized*. This means that they have been learned so well and usually at such an early age that they have been ingrained as habit. This does not mean you are stuck with the learned emotional responses (anymore than you are stuck with your learned bad spending habits) *if you choose to change them*.

Why bother changing emotional responses? Because we are often victimized by them—meaning that we have programmed responses to emotions such as:

fear: fly **or** fight
sadness: feel pain **or** go into denial & shock
anger: aggression **or** repression.

These on-off reactions are not real *choices*. They are reflexes. **Reflexes are choiceless.** Living stress free is all about freedom and that means having a *choice* (or two or three or four . . .).

Four Truths About Emotions

If you wish to have more control over your emotional responses it is necessary to internalize the following truths about emotions:

1. You Must Own Your Emotions to Control Them

Yes, here we are back to that passionate possession first step of Primary Domino Thinking again! Stop blaming others for **your** emotional responses; it is **your** expectations that set you up for **your** emotional responses anyway. Empowering yourself means owning your emotional responses in order to have healthy control over them.

2. Emotions Are Not Verdicts About You

Genetics or early instruction programmed your emotional responses into you. Everybody has emotions, whether they exhibit them or not or whether they like them or not. A particular emotion can never declare you a "bad" person. Emotions are not evil or animalistic.

3. Emotions Can Be Felt Without Being Acted Upon

Just because you feel an emotion does not mandate that you have to automatically express it.

It can be a conscious choice **if** and **how** you express a felt emotion.

4. Resisting the Experiencing of Your Emotions Guarantees They Will Persist in Running Your Life

Suppressed feelings do not go away. Energy cannot be created or destroyed—neither can emotions since they are definitely a form of energy! Resisted emotions will either explode into action after a period of time and/or they will come out "sideways," e.g., *sarcasm* is sideways anger; *whining* is anger coming through a smaller hole; *sobbing* is refusing to cry (crying is done with the eyes, not the throat); *boredom* is refraining from feeling your feelings altogether.

Another way emotions come out sideways is through psychosomatic illnesses as mentioned in the section on distress in Chapter One. How this works is that if you eat your feelings by consciously suppressing them, or unconsciously repressing or denying them, you store them not only in your mind but also in your body *somewhere*. To lock emotions into your tissues does not feel good. Ever have a stiff neck? Headaches? Lower back ache? Leg cramps? That's just physical phraseology for unresolved emotional business stored in body tissues. In other words, "You can run, but you can't hide" from your emotions.

13

Identifying Emotions

Most of our decisions are based, to a great extent, on the emotions we are experiencing at the time. Often, however, we may not be exactly aware of the emotions present in us at that particular moment. The **A–Z Emotions List** exercise next will illustrate this point.

The **A–Z Emotions List** you are about to view is the largest and most comprehensive list of emotionally related words presently available. I compiled it for 12 years until it now boasts a count of over 600! [Please, do **not** mail me any more!]

Now and then I would utilize the list with clients, particularly if they seemed "stuck" or emotionless, listless, or depressed to the point that they could not identify their feelings. For example, I might start out by saying, "How are you feeling?" and they would either say "I don't know" or "I'm not sure" or something similar. I would then hand them the list with a pencil and tell them to read the list (it was shorter then) and circle the ones that seemed active in their lives lately. It was interesting to watch clients start out apathetically then, as they were "grabbed" by a certain word, watch them grind the pencil around a word and mutter something like, "'Disappointed'? I would say I'm disappointed alright!" The List never failed in revealing repressed emotions.

After the client did some circling we would have no shortage of things to discuss. Before they would leave I would always ask them, "Remember when you came in and I asked you how you were feeling and you said, 'I don't know.'" [Then it would go something like this:] They would nod. "Then you did the list and circled all those feeling-words?" They would nod. "Where do you think those feelings were?" They would shrug. I would answer for them, "Inside you! They were 'stored' because they were suppressed, repressed, or denied. [pause] Stop doing that!" They would nod. We might have to repeat this scenario for a few weeks until they got it—then I couldn't get a word in edgewise after that!

Don't feel like I am saying these people, or you, are stupid because we are not in touch with our feelings. We are methodically, and often deliberately trained to suppress our emotions. We're just good learners! Me, too! When my teachers along the way said pay attention to your feelings I stared at them and said, "Of course!" but, didn't have a clue! The lessons from denial are often painful and make you definitely feel as if you are "a taco short of a combo dinner" besides! BUT: there is hope, dear one!

 If my past programming has determined my choices up until now, then my current choices can determine my future programming!

But first, as always, *awareness is the key!* So, now it's your turn to get aware of your feelings.

Read through the following list with a pencil circling words that are descriptive of your feelings. You may be surprised at how many there are!

The A–Z Emotions List

From the list circle the ones that are currently in your life. In the space to the right, pen a couple of words that identify the event/issue from which this particular feeling is emanating. This will take a few minutes.

Example:
anxiety: *looking foolish learning this new computer application at work*

abandoned
absorbed
abused
adamant
adequate
adored
adventurous
affectionate
afraid
aggravated
aghast
agitation
agonized
alarm
alert
alienated
alive
almighty
alone
aloof
amazed
ambivalent
amiable
ambitious
amorous
amused

angry
anguish
animated
animosity
annoyance
annoyed
anticipation
antsy
anxious
apathetic
appreciative
apprehensive
artificial
artistic
ashamed
assured
astonished
attached
attractive
aversion
aware
awed
awesome
awful
awkward
bad
bashful
beat
beautiful
belittled
betrayed
bewildered
bitchy
bitter
blah
blissful
bloated

blown up
blue
bold
bored
brave
breathless
broken-hearted
bubbly
bugged
bumbling
bummed-out
buoyant
burdened
burdensome
burned up
burned-out
calculating
calm
capable
captivated
cared for
carefree
caring
certain
chagrined
challenged
changed
charmed
charming
cheated
cheerful
churlish
childish
chipper
clammy
clean
clever

close
cold
combative
comfortable
comforted
compatible
competitive
complete
composed
committed
concerned
condemned
condescending
confident
confused
connected
consoled
conspicuous
contented
contrite
cooking
cool
courageous
cowardly
cozy
crabby
cramped
cranky
crappy
crashed-and-burned
crazy
credulous
crispy
critical
cross
cruel
crummy

crushed
cuddly
curious
cute
cutoff
daffy
dainty
damned
dandy
dangling
daring
dazed
dazzled
deceitful
defeated
defensive
definite
dehumanized
degraded
dejected
delighted
depressed
desirous
desolate
despair
despairing
despondent
destroyed
destructive
detached
determined
devilish
diabolical
different
dignified
diligent
diminished

disappointed
disconnected
discouraged
disgruntled
disgusted
disheartened
disinterested
dislike
disloyal
dismayed
disoriented
displeased
disquieted
dissatisfied
distant
distracted
distraught
distressed
disturbed
divided
dominated
dopey
doubtful
down
drained
dread
dubious
ducky
dull
dumb
eager
ecstatic
eerie
efficient
elated
electrified
elegant
embarrassed

embittered
emotional
emotionally-drained
empty
enchanted
encouraged
energetic
engrossed
enhanced
enjoyment
enlivened
enthusiastic
envious
evil
exalted
exasperated
exceptional
excited
exhausted
exhilarated
expansive
expectant
exposed
exuberant
failing
false
fanatical
fascinated
fatigued
fearful
feminine
fenced-in
fidgety
filthy
flaky
flustered
foolish

forgotten
forlorn
fragile
frantic
free
fried
friendly
frightened
frivolous
frustrated
fulfilled
full
funny
furious
gallant
gentle
glad
gloomy
good
good-humored
goofy
graceful
grateful
gratified
great
greedy
grief
grossed out
groove
growing
grumpy
guilty
gullible
haggard
happy
hassled
hate

hateful
heavenly
heavy
helpful
helpless
hesitant
high
homesick
honored
hopeful
hopeless
horny
horrible
horrified
hostile
hot
humble
humdrum
humiliated
hurt
hypercritical
hypnotized
hypocritical
hysterical
icky
ignored
immature
immortal
impatient
imposed-upon
impressed
incompetent
complete
independent
indifferent
industrious
inept

inert
infatuated
infuriated
inhuman
inquisitive
insecure
insensitive
inspired
insufficient
intense
interested
intimate
intimidated
intrigued
invigorated
involved
irate
irked
irritable
irritated
isolated
jealous
jittery
jostled
joyful
joyous
jubilant
jumpy
keen
keyed-up
kicky
kind
kinky
knowledgeable
kooky
laid-back
languid

lassitude
lazy
leery
left-out
let-down
lethargic
lewd
lifted-up
lighthearted
listless
lonely
loose
longing
lost
lousy
lovable
loving
low
loyal
lucky
lustful
mad
magnanimous
manipulated
masculine
mature
mean
melancholy
mellow
merry
mesmerized
middle-aged
mirthful
mischievous
miserable
misgiving
misunderstood

modest
moody
mopey
morbid
mortal
mortified
mournful
moved
naive
natural
naughty
nauseated
neat
negative
neglected
nervous
neutral
nice
nutty
obnoxious
obsessed
odd
offended
old
opposed
optimistic
organized
out-on-a-limb
out-of-control
out-of-sorts
outraged
overjoyed
overwhelmed
pacified
pain
panicky
patronizing

peaceful
peachy
peeved
perplexed
persecuted
pessimistic
petrified
phony
picked-on
pissed-off
pity
pleasant
pleased
poor
possessed
positive
pressures
pretty
prim
protected
protective
proud
provoked
punished
purged
puzzled
quarrelsome
quiet
radiant
rattled
reassured
refreshed
rejected
relaxed
reliable
relieved
reluctant

remorseful
repelled
repulsed
resentful
reserved
responsible
responsive
restless
restricted
reverent
rewarded
rich
righteous
rotten
rude
sad
satisfied
scared
scatter-brained
scrappy
screwed
screwed up
scruffy
scummy
secure
self-sufficient
selfish
sensitive
serene
settled
sexy
shaky
shallow
shitty
shocked
shy
sick

silly
singed
skeptical
skuzzy
sleepy
smart
sneaky
snugly
soft
solemn
sorrowful
sorry
sour
spacey
special
spellbound
spiritless
spiteful
splendid
squelched
squeamish
squirmy
squirrelly
startled
sticky
stimulated
stingy
strange
strong
stuck-up
stuffed
stunned
stupefied
stupid
supercharged
sure
surly

surprised
suspicious
sweet
sympathetic
tactful
talkative
tearful
tempted
tenacious
tender
tenderness
tense
tepid
terrible
terrified
thankful
threatened
thrilled
ticked
timid
thwarted
tired
torn
touched
tranquil
trapped
troubled
trusted
trusting
ugly
uncertain
uncomfortable
unconcerned
undignified
uneasy
uneducated
unfinished

unglued
unhappy
uninterested
unique
unnerved
unreal
unsettled
unsteady
unwholesome
upset
uptight
used
useless
vehement
vigilant
violent
vital
vivacious
vulnerable
wacky
warm
wary
weak
weary
weepy
weird
whole
wicked
wide-awake
wistful
witchey
withdrawn
woeful
wonderful
worried
wounded
wretched

yielding
young
yucky
zany
zapped
zealous
zippy

Q: Just where **were** those feelings before you recognized them on the list?
A: _____[Correct! Stored,
unresolved, **inside you!**

Insight Exercise

Review all circled words to see if there is a pattern.
Did you circle mostly

- Mad
- Sad
- Glad, or
- Fearful

words? Is there a clue here? Write about your
insights:

_____
_____
_____
_____
_____
_____
_____
_____
_____
_____

14

Communicating Feelings

Well, now that you have identified some feelings, wouldn't it be nice to have a *safe* means of communicating them? You need to let people know how experiences are affecting you but not offend, threaten, or expose others in the process. That's what I mean by "safe."

Here's a nice little emotional communication formula that works well.

When _____ *(happens)*
It makes me _____
And I feel _____.

This removes the "blame spin" from what you are saying. This prevents defensiveness on the part of the listener. The last thing (besides violence) you want in a conversation is defensiveness. *Defensiveness* is just another word for "This conversation is officially over!" In order to have *effective communication* (meaning it does at least some good) you must intend to keep the channels open.

Here's some samples of how the little emotional communication formula works:

When: you don't listen to me
It makes me: seem insignificant
And I feel: hurt.

When: I get passed over for a promotion
It makes me: wonder if I am useful here
And I feel: confused.

When: I cook a great meal and nobody says anything
It appears that: I am taken for granted
And I feel: irritated.

Notice that the last one is modified slightly. You can do that! There's no strict rule here. The point is to: a) be clear; b) own the feelings; and, c) prevent defensiveness. So, remembering to use the *I* pronoun a lot more than the *You* pronoun is a good rule of thumb for keeping the channels of communication open.

Try it for a while until it becomes natural. It works wonders.

Suppression

Why is it so important to know your own feelings and communicate your emotions? *Suppression,* or "stuffing" of feelings, is usually not healthy for adults. As children we learned how to do this because perhaps there was a penalty for not doing it—maybe we heard people saying things back to us such as:

"I'll give you something to be mad about, Buster!" (when we exhibited anger),

"You have nothing to feel sad about. Stop feeling sorry for yourself!" (when we exhibited sadness), or

"What are you afraid of, you big chicken!" (when we exhibited fear).

In other words we were threatened or shamed for having honest emotions so we developed means of "eating our feelings" in order to be safe.

Now, as adults, we have to unlearn this habit by knowing that it is safe to, first, identify and, second, talk about our feelings. In this manner we get to enjoy having that juice of emotion back in our lives. There are enough stressors in daily life without creating more through unnecessary storage of unresolved emotions.

Because emotions have a physical as well as a mental component, many of the methods in the next section are also helpful in dealing effectively with your feelings.

III
PHYSICAL TOOLS

15

Conscious Connected Breathing

Stress is found in your body in the form of muscular "tension." I have mentioned that many adults grow up "armored," resulting in habitually tense muscle groups in their bodies. Sooner or later these areas will become distressed (damaged). Due to withdrawn attention those areas become "life-force neglected." This means that those areas will not get the movement, circulation, and relaxation necessary for healthy functioning. This will eventually result in impairment - usually serious enough to cause painful, permanent, or even terminal damage. Several tools are highly effective in remedying this situation—all of which are preferable to using CONSTANT TENSION as a technique!

Conscious Connected Breathing

One of the primary signs of life is whether you are breathing or not. Breath is more significant to your life than water, sunlight, or food. If you need proof, ask yourself this question: "Of breath, water, sunlight, or food, which am I willing to go an hour without?"

Breathing has another significant function: It is a physically obvious barometer read by your subconscious mind in an ongoing evaluation of

135

your current life situation. When we feel threatened we hold our breath or breathe shallowly. (Notice the way you breathe the next time you are balancing your checkbook!) On the other hand, when we feel at peace, such as watching a beautiful sunset or experiencing "afterglow," we breathe fully and slowly.

Breathing is also unique in that it is a bodily function that can be done consciously or unconsciously. Years can go by without your deliberately controlling your breathing and still survive even if you sleep or faint or are knocked out. But you can also make a conscious choice to change your breathing pattern to benefit you. We just never knew there was a benefit to deliberately altering our breathing patterns!

Since your autonomic nervous system reads your "body language"—especially your mode of breathing—to see if there is cause for alarm (and a subsequent fight or flight response) it is in your best interests to breathe slowly and fully as often as you can remember to do so. This type of breathing sends a physiological message of serenity to your muscles, circulatory system, and glands (even if you **are** in a stressful situation). Most of us, however, have grown up doing shallow and disconnected breathing—constantly sending a message of panic to the blind autonomic system —resulting in unnecessary distress upon our systems.

Learn to breathe like a baby-at-peace naturally does. It is one of the most powerful forms of instant stress management in the world—and you always have it at your disposal (unless you are face down in the tub without a snorkel!).

There are two simple and powerful guidelines for breathing to your maximum benefit:

1. Connect the inhale and exhale *at both ends,* i.e., keep the breathing totally circular.

2. Relax the exhale, i.e., refrain from controlling the exhale with your stomach, chest, throat or lips. Just let the air come out of its own accord.

Practice this right now with your eyes closed for five straight minutes. Notice after about thirty seconds (when you begin to feel good) how your mind wants you to get busy with something else. This is an example of how we like to rain on our own parade!

Conscious Connected Breathing Guidelines

a) You may become dizzy the first few times you do Conscious Connected Breathing, so don't take in quite so much air if it gets uncomfortable. If you like being dizzy, breathe deeper! (This is why, until you get used to it, you shouldn't operate heavy machinery while doing CCB.)

b) Do CCB whenever you think of it. It is especially helpful in times of tension: getting a speeding ticket; before a job interview; facing your boss; arguing with your (or anybody's) spouse; waiting at a railroad crossing or in line when you are in a hurry; and, worrying about anything else in the universe.

c) CCB is a great way to return to dreamland if you wake up in the middle of the night and restlessly cannot go back to sleep by the usual means of pounding your pillow and screaming inside your head, "I've **got** to get some sleep!" Even if CCB doesn't always restore you to sleep, you will be so relaxed you won't care.

d) CCB is a great way to start your day. **Get up** 5 minutes earlier than usual, **sit up** so you don't go back to sleep, and **do it** (CCB). Notice the difference in your morning!

e) Slow and full breathing is the most peaceful. If you are afraid or angry and cannot seem to get a lot of air, at least keep your breathing connected until you can breathe more deeply.

f) It is very important to follow the two guidelines. You'll get better with practice, so do it often.

Note: Now that you know how to breathe correctly, take the Stress Test in Appendix I. It will help you to a) assess where you are today with regard to stressors; and, b) to see clearly the connection between unresolved stress and physical illness.

16

Guided Imagery

Guided imagery is directing your attention consciously in a planned pattern to:

a) maximize effectiveness for general relaxation and tension reduction; or

b) rehearse an upcoming high-pressure situation so as to minimize non-productive stress.

Relaxation and Tension Reduction

Part 1. Sit erect or lie flat on your back if you can and, with hands at your side and legs uncrossed, begin to tense and then relax every muscle group in your body.

- First tense your feet and legs as tight as you can for three seconds and then relax for three seconds
- Repeat with the same muscle group

Then follow the same pattern of tensing and relaxing for three seconds *twice* with the following muscle groups in sequence:

- buttocks and lower back muscles (pinch your buns together)

- stomach and chest muscles
  (hold your breath here and *tighten up*)
- hands and arms
  (clench your fists)
- back muscles
  (bring your angel wings together)
- neck and shoulder muscles
  (be a turtle and pull your head in)
- jaw muscles
  (clench your teeth)
- facial muscles
  (squinch your face up)
- ear and scalp muscles
  (raise your ears and frown)

Remember to tighten and loosen each of these areas twice, then just lie there for a while and do CCB.

Practice this now if you're somewhere that you can lie down (or make a commitment to do it ASAP, OK?) Nod your head if you agree.

Part 2. Now that your body is fairly, if not completely, relaxed, let's keep it that way while we do some imagery. With your eyes closed imagine the inside of your forehead is a white screen—like being parked in the front row before the drive-in movie starts. Visualize the white screen becoming a friendly fog bank that wraps around you and relaxes you even more. Do this for about a minute. Image the fog clearing away before a gently warming sun above your head. As the fog clears completely away find yourself in the middle of a huge tree-encircled private meadow with golden grass blowing gently in the breeze. Visualize yourself lying in the warm and dry meadow, with the sun warming your skin, muscles, and bones—until your whole body is toasty warm and feels comfortably heavy. Smell the grass; hear birds chirping in the distance; and, notice the golden glow of the sun through your eyelids, as you breathe deeply and connectedly with relaxed exhales. Do this for five minutes. In your mind's eye stand up and notice your outline in the grass. Look around and take in the details of this special place. Remember it well so that you can easily return here whenever you feel troubled, worried, tense, afraid, restless, or need to gather your energies.

Relaxation Imagery Tips

a) Try trips to the mountains, seashore, outer space, and other favorite relaxing spots you might like. Only your imagination limits you—and your imagination is unlimited!

b) If it's too hectic to lie down, just closing your eyes for a few seconds and taking a few deep breaths while remembering your secret hideaway can help a great deal. Try it in the elevator, in line, at the office, or anywhere except while driving or peeling vegetables (and especially not while driving *and* peeling vegetables!).

Rehearsal of Stressful Event

Part 1. [Same as Part 1 above]

Part 2. Visualize the interior white screen and see yourself in the upcoming situation that you are concerned about. Notice how your body and your facial expressions appear as you feel the emotions that you are dreading. Really feel this as if it was happening for about one minute. Now begin to see your self handling the situation with total confidence. Focus your consciousness into how you would look and feel (it is very important to **feel** the emotions that go with the pictures) if everything went better than you could ever expect. Now notice how your body language and facial expression is more relaxed and pleasant. Do this over and over until you notice yourself feeling permanently assured about the anticipated event.

Rehearsal Imagery Tips

a) Worry does not create positive results. If that were true all of us who worry about money would be billionaires! Anxiety is destructive when you cannot focus your consciousness or energies onto healthy or progressive alternatives long enough to produce effective solutions for your dilemma. Visualizing yourself as dynamically handling the problem "cools you out" enough to really do just that! For decades nationally competitive athletes have used this to increase their performance.

b) Thoughts are powerful because all action is preceded by thought. What you think about is pretty much a flight plan being filed for your future. Remember: **What you focus on expands.** If you focus on anxiety it will grow and grow. If you focus on serenity **it** will grow and grow. Preferences, anyone?

c) At first it takes conscious effort (work) to reverse our old ways of thinking. This

c) At first it takes conscious effort (work) to reverse our old ways of thinking. This means a period of deliberate willingness and practice to make it happen. Give it a go—after a while **you will feel that life works for you instead of feeling like you have to work for a living!**

17

Physical Exercise

No book on stress management would be complete without mentioning the benefits of physical exercise. Healthy exercise is one of the finest stress "relievers," as opposed to stress "eliminators," i.e., it doesn't do much to alleviate the source of the stress, but it goes a long way in alleviating some of the symptoms.

We accumulate a lot more stress than we can effectively process due to our compacted schedules and demanding lifestyles—and a scanty "toolbox" doesn't help the situation either! A vigorous exercise program performed properly can take care of the impact of many hidden stresses. [Note: It is always important to get medical advice prior to making sudden and dramatic changes in exercise regimens.]

Five Reasons Why Exercise Is Helpful

1. You actually force the muscular tissues in which you store unresolved stress to surrender their tense state by making them move, thereby improving oxygenation and circulation in those areas.

2. You remove yourself from the source of your stress while performing exercise: A mini-vacation!

3. Your mind is free from preoccupying responsibilities to come up with creative solutions to some of your problems.

4. As your exercise program takes hold, your self-image, confidence, and determination improve.

5. You will have more energy, a healthier appetite, a better sex life, sleep better and find it easier to maintain your ideal weight.

So, get going!

Here are just a few great forms of exercise:

Swimming	Hiking	Tennis
Biking	Racquetball	Dance
Walking	Skating	Jogging
Aerobics	Skiing	Calisthenics
Weightlifting	Surfing	Rollerblading

Not meeting my Guideline a) below and therefore deliberately **not** mentioned in the above list:

Darts	Television	Gardening
Bowling	Shopping	Billiards
Bingo	Golf	Draining the dog

Guidelines for Healthy Exercise

a) Work up to at least 30 minutes of **sustained** exercise with increased heart rate three times weekly on the average. Break a sweat, breathe heavy a little and **feel good about that.**

b) Don't overdo it . . . we're relieving stress here, not trying to find yet another expression of compulsivity.

c) Of course, there is *no time* for fitness! We must talk priorities, priorities, priorities, my friend! The way of the world is erosion. Without intervention we humans erode as we get older. This is not a fun prospect. If you become too stressed, too sick, or too out of condition you will not have any resources left to do anything with anyway . . . so, get real and prioritize for exercise!

It does take willingness and effort to break out of your non-productive comfort zone (inertia), but: **Consider the consequences of procrastination.** There are always consequences for prolonged inactivity, and quite a few of those are nasty. Don't be lulled by the gradualness of the build-up into complacency and/or acclimation to slothfulness. Remember that suicide can be quick, or on the installment plan, but it's still suicide. Love yourself more than this. Remember, if you don't care about you, who will?

18

Play

I remember in the 60's reading that in the 80's people would be working a 4-day-week, and if you wanted to be cleverly futuristic in career planning you should prepare for a job in the field of Recreation & Leisure. Latest statistics from 1996 show that people were averaging over 44 hours a week at work and spending at least half of their weekend working around the house or at a second source of income. Wonder what all those recreation specialists are doing with **their** free time these days?

Today we are so committed to careers, social activities, and family and civic responsibilities that we are not leaving any time even on weekends for our brains and bodies to recuperate. Is it possible that weekends are becoming as stressful as our work week? If trends continue, work might eventually become the place where we have the least stress! Is this becoming true for you? This could become a serious condition if we don't remember to take time to **play.** Remember what it feels like to play?

Six Tips on Learning How to Play

Here are some helpful tips on how to relearn how to play:

1. Confront the Guilt About Taking Time to Play

Playing, relaxing and having fun are healthy activities in and of themselves. As an adult you don't have to justify your use of time to that little drill sergeant in your head anymore. Give the Sarge a day off as well!

2. Keep Work and Play Separate

Don't pretend ignorance here. Talking shop after hours is still "being at work." Playing golf with the boss or clients is clearly still not "play." Social events where one doesn't have to be vigilant are much more conducive to recreation and recuperation that when one has to be "on best behavior."

3. Expand Your Leisure Horizons

Spontaneity is a key component of play. If your leisure activities have become routine then you are missing that refreshing ingredient. Set aside at least one day a month where you try something different. We are afraid of change, and we don't like doing something in which we might be awkward, but as G.B. Shaw stated:

"A man learns to ice skate by staggering around making a fool of himself. Indeed, we progress in all things by resolutely making fools of ourselves."

Teaching courses on human growth & development and dysfunctional family issues, combined with my psychotherapy practice, has provided some interesting insights into the human condition. One of those insights applies here rather well. It became obvious to me that one of the big penalties for people trying new experiences is the fear of appearing "silly" or being seen as "weird" or something other than what we have come to call *normal*. Where do all prevalent hang-ups originate? Having been an observer of parent-child and teacher-child interactions over the years because of my academic interests, I often see the power of these situations on children's development right in front of me at grocery stores, on the street, in malls, restaurants, etc.

There are four things nobody wants to be called:

Ugly

Lazy

Stupid

and worst of all

Crazy

I have noticed that there are clearly huge penalties from caregivers and authority figures for being "different" in our society. And it's as childhood contagious as a kindergarten cold! Soon, one's school peers are making social outcasts of kids who do not conform to the trends/standards of the group. Research shows that if the parents, teachers and preachers couldn't shape you up the peer group usually could, and then they continue to do so **until death do us part.**

4. Refuse to Turn Play into Work

Everything doesn't have to be a goal-oriented endeavor. The key is to stay absorbed in the moment playing like a child. Too many of us turn hobbies and sports into tasks to be worked at. When I first took up jogging it was really "running," watching my time, trying to better it everyday (and getting up sore as hell the next morning!) and beginning to dread it. Today I jog without a watch and just mindlessly enjoy the scenery and my breathing.

5. Find New Playmates

If you always spend your free time with the same circle of friends you'll probably always do the same activities. Rest and relaxation means moderation, **not** boredom. Be on the lookout for new potential friends. I have a friend who now and then goes on a deliberate "people hunt" just to freshen up his social pool of possible acquaintances.

6. Stop Putting It Off

If we put off enjoying our free time for too long we may never find the right moment to savor it. Remember:

 *Enjoy life **now**, this is not a dress rehearsal.*

"Doing something constructive" (what we were all admonished to do since childhood) can be something besides making money, doing your "duty," or home improvements.

Just as constructive: Spend at least 4 hours a weekend having fun.

Just as constructive: Make it a goal to do something that will create wonderful memories.

Just as constructive: Refrain from working on holidays—celebrate!

All of us kids, the small ones **and** the big ones, need regular recess.

19

Time Management

Well, let's not kid around here. Your *time* is your life. Remember the dedication of the book?

[You didn't read it? Please read it now, OK?]

For all of you who believe you are going to die, on your tombstone your whole life-*time* is a simple little line: —. Your life is certainly not valuable to the stonecutter when he chisels it, and obviously not to the original dash designer: What the heck kind of dignity is there in a dash, anyway?

> *"Time deals gently only with those*
> *who take it gently."*
> —Anatole France

> *"Time makes more converts than reason."*
> —Thomas Paine

> *"In season, all is good."*
> —Sophocles

> *"That it will never come again*
> *is what makes life so sweet."*
> —Emily Dickenson

> *"As if you could kill time*
> *without injuring eternity."*
> —Henry David Thoreau

To be highly effective with *time management* one must know *why* one is going to do what is being contemplated. A *mission statement* does not exist to impress people. It is a guiding light, a meter stick to help you measure your possible future expenditures of energy. A mission statement is also a confidence builder in that you will always know when you are on the right track—a major stress-reliever in and of itself.

Discovering Your Life's Mission

If you do not know your mission, then your life will not be determined by you. Not to worry, people will, of course, find a use for you. But if you do not know your mission, you will adopt theirs since any purpose is better than no purpose. Unfortunately, this means that you will not feel very fulfilled and patterns of low self-esteem will surely permeate your life. Without a sense of mission you have only the alternatives of conformity or rebellion, neither of which is deeply satisfying.

There is an alternative to conformity or rebelliousness: Self-directedness. A self-directed person knows his or her own mission and does not look to other people for definition. Only through self-directedness can fulfillment be found. The rebel and conformist are always plagued by profound questions about whether they are doing the right thing with their lives. The self-directed person is empowered and experiences certainty.

It is also extremely difficult to make any major decision in a meaningful way without knowing your mission. Compared to knowing what your mission is, all other decisions are trivial. Your purpose is not something that you achieve once and then you are finished; it is something you express continuously, giving meaning to goals throughout your life. Your mission puts your entire life into perspective.

If you do not know your mission, you can discover it by performing the following process.

1. If you had the power to make your world any way at all, how would you choose it to be? Reflect a few minutes, then write this down in 20 words or less, utilizing positive language entirely. _____

    _____

    _____

    _____

    _____

    _____

2. Make List #1: 10 things you like about yourself in noun-based language. [my good looks; my speaking ability; my ability to memorize; etc.]

    1._____

    2._____

    3._____

    4._____

    5._____

    6._____

    7._____

    8._____

    9._____

    10. _____

3. From List #1 circle 3 or 4 that are the most significant about you.

4. Make List #2: Ten activities you enjoy engaging in as an expression of the 3 or 4 things you listed above. These should be

gerunds ending in -ing. [singing; debating with politicians; painting; cooking; presenting ideas; etc.]

1._____
2._____
3._____
4._____
5._____
6._____
7._____
8._____
9._____
10. _____

6. From List #2 circle 3 or 4 that can make the biggest contribution to making the world more like the ideal you described in Step One.

7. Create your Mission by writing out the following sentence, filling in the blanks with the selection from List #1, then List #2, then your ideal world.

"My Mission is to use my _____, _____, and _____, by _____ing, _____ing, and _____ing so that:

_____
_____
_____
_____
_____."

8. Polish your grammar until your statement makes good sense to you.

Don't worry if your Mission doesn't seem to exactly fit you at first. This is not unusual. It helps to do this every day for a week until you feel in your heart that "This is it!" Remember, this is an experience concerned with the trajectory of your life, so be willing to take your time and get it just right for you.

I strongly suggest you utilize this process for any important projects in which you decide to invest your energy. It will make your projects more meaningful, enjoyable, enthusiastic and effective because you will be clear about what you are doing and why. Most importantly, you will be at cause rather than at effect, which is how you were designed to be.

The mission statement is your true North on your life's compass, guiding you through meaninglessness, confusion, difficult decisions, and allocation of your valuable resources such as time, money, energy, emotions, and relationships.

One of my favorite stories about how a mission statement transformed someone's life was a friend of mine who was feeling somewhat depressed— had that blues "Just-what-AM-I-going-to-do-with-my-life!" tone to it. I encouraged her to do the mission statement exercise and, although typically reluctant at first, she came up with this beauty:

My mission is to manifest peace, serenity and harmony in the world by filling spaces with gardening, cooking and creating beautiful things.

What is particularly interesting about this woman and her mission statement is that at first she took it as a very external activity-oriented guidance system. She dove into her activities with cookbooks and seed catalogs and all the tools thereof, only to discover that her new mission statement had a great deal of relevance for her thoughts as well. From that time on a lot of her "gardening" was internal self-examination such that the garden in the space between her ears also began to reflect the beauty, harmony and serenity of her mission statement.

   As within, so without.

20

How to Prioritize

Now that you have a mission statement (you do, don't you?), prioritizing is much easier. When you must decide what to do with your time, money, energy, or other resources, ask yourself, "Does this align itself with my mission?" If the answer is "Yes!" then jump in, or at least put it on top of your list for future pouncing upon. If the answer is "No!" then either put in no resources, or as little as you can get by with. (Nothing is wrong with minimizing effort—it's called *economy.*) If the answer is, "I don't know" then you need to get more information **before** making a decision to find out which pile it belongs in.

How to Prioritize People

Yep, you really must learn how to prioritize the time you spend with people! Unfortunately, most stressors are caused by those representatives of the human race called "people." If you don't believe me look at the stress test in the Appendix and you'll see that 8 of the top 10 stressors are because of relationships. And for the life of me, I am still mystified why so many of us feel obligated to put up with those people who stress us on a regular basis. I have yet to see many rewards given for social martyrdom so I guess it must be a bad habit!

I promised you I would cut to the chase on a lot of these issues, so here goes: People are divided into two piles:

1. Those you will associate with; and,

2. Those you will not associate with.

For example, there are people in Hong Kong *you will never even see* much less *meet,* right? There are people in your country, state, or even town that you will never meet. There are people you never met who are dead as well, right? There are tons and tons of people you have never met, can't meet, and will never meet. Do you feel guilty about that? Of course not.

So what is the big deal about deliberately placing people in that pile? If someone is really obnoxious, irritating, or denigrates you in any way, you can even tell them to their face with no explanation, "Hey, Buster, you know what? You just went into the other pile!" Then turn on your heel, walk away and never look back!

If these "other pile" occupants are in your family or you have to work with them and there seems to be no way to negotiate a more pleasant relationship, minimize not only your physical association with them as much as possible, but don't argue or talk with them, talk about them, or even think about them any more than you absolutely must. **Take charge of those who are attempting to walk through your head wearing muddy boots!**

Make a list of muddy boot wearers that you need to start taking action with: _____

_____

_____

_____

_____

_____

_____

_____

_____

_____

How to Prioritize Energy with Things That Deplete You

 Learn how to pick your fights!

Is the experience I am facing at this moment **that** important to continue engaging in it? Is this argument, decision, conversation, problem, event, experience, etc., conducive to my *wealth* ("wealth" is anything that promotes growth, development, health or happiness—and that includes $$$!) or not? Yes or No? If it is, continue. If not, disengage as quickly and courteously as possible and get on to something that *does*. [Boy, is this prioritizing stuff simple or what?]

Okay, sometimes it's a little tougher than this, and that's almost always caused by one of the following issues. I'll supply some formulated responses.

Problems with Prioritizing

Confusion

Perhaps at this particular moment you cannot decide if this argument, decision, conversation, problem, event, experience, etc., is going to be conducive to your wealth or not. Perhaps the issue appears too complex, or issues are too hazy.

Response: Hang in there with an open and inquisitive mind with the strict purpose of gathering more information until you can make a decision.

Obligation

You have made a commitment to engage in this particular work, family, etc., activity, and now things no longer seem that beneficial to your *wealth* (growth, development, health or happiness).

Response: Renegotiate the terms of your engagement as soon as is feasible. Inform people that your needs are not being met or that the situation is counterproductive for you and new terms need to be drawn up. If renegotiation is not possible, and/or other participants are unwilling, hang in there long enough to fulfill your sense of obligation, but start looking around actively for new opportunities.

Painful Consequences

Are you in a place where you will be made to suffer if you decide to go with your top priorities?

Are you stuck, hemmed in, prevented, or even threatened from exercising your top priorities?

Response: This is a dangerous situation, and you need to begin seeking alternative routes right away. Just by *starting* to look for a way out is a major stress reliever, because at least you are **doing** something proactively rather than just settling for **endurance as a strategy.** Maybe you need help? In most communities you are at best only two phone calls from support or protection. For right now your top priority should be yourself.

If you aren't safe, healthy, or free, what good are you to anyone? Don't hesitate, Okay?

Lack of Stamina

A common problem in determining priorities is even the lack of stamina to do so. Some people are, as my Grandma from Mobile used to say, "Plum wore out." Being "wore out" can be from several causes, most notably fatigue and/or depression. If you are chronically too limp, depleted, wrung out, or whatever, do I have good news for you!

Response: This is a serious condition. You must now give yourself top priority for renewing your energy supply. There are two paths:

a) You must get away for a while to restore your energy. I am talking about going somewhere *alone* and remaining very *unbusy* for at least two days if not more. Most everyone can claim two days for himself or herself if they really want to. If you are "wore out" you really don't have a choice but to do this. Otherwise you are killing yourself, and, fortunately for you, that goes against the theme of this book, and your and my partnership!

I have recommended this to people often and they have made arrangements for having their work/kids/pets/house/etc., taken care of and gone to a cabin, a friend's vacant home, a retreat center, or even checked into a motel for two nights (one night is not enough!). Stay away from television, telephones, people, shopping, etc., and just have some quiet time to sleep, reflect, write, meditate, pray, **rest,** and recuperate. Not one person has ever come back from one of these and said, "What a crappy idea that was!" Quite the contrary, it has worked miracles. Give yourself this gift if you're "Plum wore out." You will return with a much clearer picture of your priorities and the energy to engage them. Promise.

b)   If you are chronically depressed (you have felt *helpless and hopeless* without let-up for 6 months or longer) get professional help. Call today. Getting counseling does not mean you are *insane.* This is an old and very inaccurate stereotype. Listen to me: ***Sane* people get help when they are hurting.** Ask around for a good counselor, preferably one experienced with depression. Usually word is out on who is effective and who is just a pill-pusher or a jerk.

21

Nutrition and Stress

As a biologist/psychologist and former owner of a health food store and restaurant I learned more about this area than I ever cared to just trying to stay ahead of my clientele's interests, as well as their fervor for the latest fad supplement, diet, nutrition/diet guru on Donahue, or scientific finding that had hit the headlines that morning.

Again, you have been beat over the head with enough information about this topic in school and from the media by now, so I am going to keep to my promise to be very to the point about this particular area of nutrition in stress management as well.

Seven Nutritional Tips

1. *Crash diets work against you.* They set you up for certain temporary failure, and worst of all, establish a pattern of long-term failure by undermining your confidence in your ability to do anything about shaping yourself in the future. Avoid them like the plague.

2. *You only have to lower your intake of calories 30 a day* **from now on—starting today.** This will take off from one to two pounds a year, thus gradually slimming you down **plus** preventing middle-age

spread! So just burn 'em off by adding another 5 minutes of exercise or cutting back on something you are eating. Do you know how little that is? Just eliminate one piece of candy, cut the cream in your coffee in half, eat half your normal dessert, etc., there are a million ways. . . . Write your commitment here:

---

3. *Take a **chelated** vitamin mineral supplement daily.* Cheap unchelated vitamins/minerals probably go through you in about the same form that they went in. Chelation makes sure they get absorbed into your system.

4. *Add fiber to your diet.* Go to your local health food store and buy a bag of wheat bran. Very cheap! Add a tablespoon a day into or onto something you eat—like cereal or fruit or in your spuds. This will keep you regular, prevent that nasty colon cancer, clean you out so you can absorb what you're supposed to absorb down there, and burn up extra calories as well. Say good-bye to constipation!

5. *Whack the excess fat.* You just gotta hang up the fried foods! Avoid them for 30 days (bite the bullet!) and then you will find it easy to stay away from them. Something soaked in oil like greasy fried chicken, or a big cheesy patty-melt may even appear repugnant to you after that! Broil and

steam your foods more, and use Pam in your pans instead of butter and margarine. Substitute applesauce for oils in your baked goods—keeps everything nice and moist and is 10 times better for you. There are some great cookbooks out there on no-fat/low-fat cooking. Buy one—read it—try it—you'll like it!

6. *Read up on allergic foods.* My store was in a town of about 35,000 people. I couldn't believe how many people had discovered they were, as an example, allergic to wheat and how their lives had changed after eliminating it from their diet. Many of their GI tract problems had vanished, along with respiratory and skin problems, general listlessness, and thought process problems. I wondered, "Wow, if this many people *know* they are allergic, how many people are ignorant of their allergies and are just living with their symptoms?" The same thing applied to dairy allergies—there were dozens of people suffering some incredible discomfort because of their inability to handle any part of milk products. And then there were all the specific allergies, such as fish, strawberries, shellfish, nuts, legumes, tomatoes, dust, molds, etc., etc.

So, get to know about this area of your life. Some of your stress could be just an allergic reaction to what you are eating, drinking or breathing, which is like shooting yourself in the foot everyday if you don't pay attention! Sometimes you can get a general indication by just deciding to deliberately notice how you feel about

5–60 minutes after you eat or inhale something. Journaling this can help as well.

7. *Alcohol and drugs are stress producers.* It is a general mind-screw to tell yourself that you *need* a drink or drug to "unwind," or that you *deserve* a drink or drug "after all you put up with." Stop conning yourself. Nothing is so bad that it can't be made worse by a mood-altering pill or another drink. Not only that but relying on chemicals prevents you from looking at more productive strategies that will build you a progressively better and healthier life.

22

First-Aid Kit:
Six Emergency
Measures

If you are in a tight spot, do one of the following instead of engaging in non-productive or even destructive coping methods. One or more of these is guaranteed to work if you work 'em.

Power-napping

Many have learned the secret of the 6–12 minute power-nap. Thomas Edison was famous for getting only about 3 hours sleep a night and then taking three or four 10 minute power-naps a day and having more energy than anyone around him. He deliberately trained himself to do this so that he could have more hours in the day to do what he wanted to do. You can do this as well, to whatever degree you wish.

The purpose of power-napping is to quickly become totally refreshed. What is most important about power-napping is that you do not oversleep. If you sleep beyond 12 minutes you will feel sluggish and even surly, because you have dipped too far into delta (deep) sleep. You will want to stay in delta sleep and be resentful if not allowed to do so, so it's best not to go there no matter how tempting. Set your alarm for 12 minutes from whenever you lie down, and **get up** when it goes off whether you have slept or not. Soon you will train yourself to "crash" almost immediately upon starting the power-nap. If you don't, just lying there and breathing consciously and connectedly helps revitalize you about 80% anyway.

Crunches

This seems strange, but when you are blue, angry, or out of sorts, try lying flat on the floor with your feet up on a chair or a bed. Put your hands behind your head and do several sets of sit-ups or stomach crunches. I believe that what happens here is that a combination of the increased heart- and breath-rate, the muscular movement, and stimulation of the nerve center known as the *solar plexus,* physically shifts the person into another frame of mind, breaking the hold of the "bad mood" cycle.

Drop a Dime

A procedure that has saved many an alcoholic from relapsing is called "dropping a dime." When the alcoholic felt the urge to drink again, he/she immediately would call someone else in the program and gain support. No reason why this won't work for you when you are ready to blow a stress-fuse (except that I think you'll need a little more than .10 cents today!).

Just call a friend and say something like this, "Hi, it's me, and I am ready to do something stupid so I thought I would do something smart and call you instead. All I need you to do is listen while I uncork. I will then hang-up and so can you. Forget I called. Thanks!" Then quickly share what's going on with you and hang up.

The Quick 20

There is an intriguing breathing pattern I call the Quick 20 that works miracles in terms of *temporarily* relieving stress and giving you a quick lift.

Try this: Without a break and relaxing the exhale—

a) Take 4 short connected breaths and one really long one.

b) Repeat 3 more times.

c) Notice how that feels.

d) Use whenever needed.

The Gratitude Lesson

The Gratitude Lesson is a first-aid technique that shifts context quickly by helping you to see in another direction that isn't so dark. Some call it *counting your blessings.*

When you feel stressors pushing you into a corner without your permission, take the reins back by quickly focussing on all the things you DO have working for you. Again, remember that what you focus on expands, so the more you deliberately concentrate on what IS working in your life, the more that will fill your consciousness with positivism.

The Fury

At first, this process will sound weird. *The Fury* is an unbelievably effective emergency measure. It is designed for **when you are at your wit's end; when you are wound too, too tight; when you are about to explode. Do *The Fury* instead!** Please follow directions **exactly**.

a) Do this alone and privately in your house, apartment or retreat. There should be no witnesses or interruptions.

b) Take off all jewelry and eyeglasses (after you read this!).

c) Place a pillow on the floor next to your bed (or couch) and kneel on it.

d) Using your forearms, **not** your fists or wrists, begin to pound on the bed, landing your forearms **flat on the bed** as hard as you can.

e) Harder.

f) As hard as you can without hurting yourself.

g) Now, begin to loudly utter the word "NO!" (unless you know a better word) as you pound.

h) Harder and louder.

i) Let whatever feelings and words come up without censoring.

j) Continue to do this until you are exhausted (it may last 10–30 minutes or more.)

k) You will experience many surprises and gain some important insights into what is eating you, if you really *let go*.

l) Rest.

m) Reflect on what you have learned.

n) Contemplate making some changes.
Journal here about what those might be:

_____

_____

_____

_____

_____

_____

_____

_____

_____

_____

_____

_____

_____

_____

_____

_____

_____

_____

_____

_____

_____

_____

_____

_____

_____

_____

_____

_____

_____

_____

_____

_____

IV

SOCIAL TOOLS

23

Relationships and Needs

We can't ignore the source of most people's stress: **relationships.** In this chapter we will focus on our interactions with others, pulling into that context some of the things we have learned before in the book, plus adding some new understandings.

Needs: Our Driving Force

Abraham Maslow, the great positivistic psychologist, so very clearly informed us of his research into what motivates people. He stated in *Motivation and Personality,* his publication on the topic, that there are six basic needs in each of us:

MASLOW'S HIERARCHY OF NEEDS

Self-Actualization Needs
↑
Self-Esteem Needs
↑
Love Needs
↑
Belongingness Needs
↑
Safety Needs
↑
Physiological Needs

These needs, he further postulated, are arranged in a hierarchical order such that the fulfillment of lower needs propels us on to the next highest level. For example, if I have a strong physiological need such as *thirst,* I will be motivated by little else, but once that need is taken care of, I will be drawn to the next level, *safety needs,* and when those are taken care of, I will move on to the third level, *belonging needs,* then the fourth, etc.

The big goal, and Maslow's fascination, was to move beyond the *deficiency needs* (the lower five were called this because they are much like your car's gas tank—always going dry!) and spend as much time as possible in the sixth, *self-actualization* of one's potentials, capacities, and talents—where you feel like you are getting some-where in your development as a person. The prob-lem was—and *is*—that the lower five levels take so much time and energy that little is left for that wondrous motivational state of self-actualization when one's spirit achieves that soaring experience of *unfolding.* Because **unresolved stressors hold you back from achieving your potential** is one excellent reason why you need to be an expert on stress management.

As your personal coach, I want you to know that in my experience one of the greatest stressors in people is the frustration of **not** actualizing their potential, of feeling like they are just "spinning their wheels and not getting anywhere" as their life slips by. If you have had enough of "wheel-spinning" and your daily accomplishments feel like merely refilling your gas tank so it can go dry again, you have another excellent reason to become an accomplished dynamic "stress-buster."

If you look closely at the lower 5 levels on Maslow's hierarchy above, you see just how much other people *are* intertwined into our lives. We rely on others to help us get our *physiological needs* of food, water, shelter, clothing, and sex met. Our *security needs* are often met in relationship with others by trust with people we do know and/or through our reliance upon social customs, mores, ethics, or the law, with people we don't know or trust. *Belongingness needs* and *love needs* are obviously met through others, and, as we discussed in an earlier section on self-esteem, our *self-esteem needs* are rooted in relationship.

So here is the **key point:** Since we have located a lot of our needs satisfaction for these five essential areas in other people, and since we cannot control people much better than a fresh watermelon seed on a Formica countertop, we have a perennial stressor production line for ourselves to make sure we never run out! No wonder so many people are frustrated with all the roadblocks in the way of self-actualization. We are so busy trying to get our needs met by other people, while they're so busy trying to get theirs met by other people, while they are so busy trying to get their needs met by other people, *ad infinitum,* that no one can be relied on to take care of ours!

BUT, there is a flaw in the trapped-factory syndrome! That flaw comes down to one deeply ingrained, **highly incorrect,** but widely held belief. Actually, it comes down to a **single erroneous word** in the following belief statement that most all of us carry around in our heads:

"I must get a particular need met by *this* person."

This outrageous belief is such an obvious pile of baloney that we miss the forest for the trees, but just a few questions bring home the obvious:

- *Why does it have to be **this** person?*
- *Did this person volunteer to be put in this position?*
- *Is he/she truly capable of delivering?*
- *Is it fair, right, or just to put this additional burden on a person already busy with their own life?*
- *What things am I going to have to do to control this person such that they deliver the goods?*

To really catch on to this, take a specific person in your life that you somehow have come to designate as your source for meeting a particular need, and answer some of the above questions. Fear not, it's just between you and me.

_____

_____

_____

_____

_____

_____

_____

_____

_____

_____

_____

_____

_____

_____

_____

_____

24

Relationships: Friends and Lovers

Intimate Relationships

I represent the concept of *intimacy* differently than most. Adults have learned to walk around in a protective bubble. We caught on in school (and, unfortunately, perhaps at home, too) that some people can hurt you when you get too close. We developed the "bubble strategy" as a means of being able to associate safely until we could determine if someone else might be safe. When we—correctly or incorrectly—decide someone else is *safe* we allow a small opening in our bubble shield to let him or her in. If they prove themselves safe, we open further and further until we have an *intimate relationship.* Characteristics of such a relationship include sharing secrets, dreams, and resources. Eventually we become *vulnerable,* meaning that we have allowed ourselves to take a *risk* that this person will care enough about us that they will be *considerate* and *sensitive* to our particular feelings and needs with the information we have dared to share.

Well, the following is probably not news to you:

Some people can't be trusted!

Here's some more non-news:

We are sometimes wrong in our assessment of just who is and who is not trustworthy.

This is how we get *burned* occasionally. Yep, it's pretty devastating when it happens, but it's not the end of the world, is it? Confession: I used to have a tendency to think it was the other person's fault when I got burned. Really! In retrospect, I can clearly see that it was my faulty judging that did me in. They were just being true to their little rascally selves, and I was *expecting* them to behave differently just for my benefit. Hee, hee, what a joke on me! I feel stupid today when I realize all this. But now you can learn from my idiocy! [Perhaps this is a good time to review *The Terrorism of Expectations* chapter.]

Another good point here is that *intimacy* has an unwritten contract included. It includes some key phrases I call SSSSR.

The Six Sacred Sacraments of Successful Relationships

We agree to:

- *trust each other*
- *respect one another*
- *be honest*
- *be open in our communicating with one another*
- *be willing to dedicate some positive energy to maintaining the relationship, and*
- *refrain from consciously abusing one another*

If you don't believe that you have always had this subconscious unspoken contract ask yourself, "Would I let myself get invested in an intimate, vulnerable relationship with someone:

- I **knowingly** could not *trust?*
- I **knew** would disrespect me?
- I **knew** would be dishonest?
- I **knew** would not communicate with me?
- I **knew** would not put anything into our relationship?
- I **knew** would deliberately abuse me?"

I certainly hope the answer was "No" to all of those. If it wasn't then you have spotted some definite areas needing work! [And keep this list around to as an aide in scoping your next intimate relationship, because you apparently need it!]

Intimate Relationships Are Voluntary

Another important thing to remember is that intimate relationships are voluntary for adults. If the contract is broken, attempt to fix it, and if it cannot (will not) be fixed, then **you have the right to cancel the whole thing.** Yes, if a relationship has begun to breach even one of the six sacraments you not only *can* but *should* immediately bring it up for:

1. inspection
2. discussion
3. resolution, and
4. possible dissolution if resolution is impossible.

Why? Because it is your *life* you have invested! It always amazes me how suspicious and careful people are with investing a few dollars, but they give big chunks of their life away as if they were worthless. Last I heard new money is being printed daily, but you only get one life.

I have heard people say, "Life is short" which I don't agree with because I have been alive as long as I can remember. You, too? BUT I do believe that **Life is precious** and nary a drop should be wasted if it can be helped. So be your own taskmaster when it comes to monitoring and care-taking your relationships. If not you, who? Start now by taking a couple of relationships prevalent in your life and running them through the SSSSR "test" by circling Yes, No or ? under each name:

	Name:_____	Name:_____
Trust	Yes No ?	Yes No ?
Respect	Yes No ?	Yes No ?
Honest	Yes No ?	Yes No ?
Open	Yes No ?	Yes No ?
Willing	Yes No ?	Yes No ?
Non-abusive	Yes No ?	Yes No ?

Any insights?

_____

_____

_____

_____

_____

_____

_____

_____

_____

Need to communicate your concern to someone?

_____
_____
_____
_____
_____
_____
_____
_____
_____
_____

Ultimate Reason to Have an Intimate Relationship

Intimate relationships are a lot of work. They are hard to find, difficult to develop, require a lot of maintenance, and are risky at best. Why bother then, right? There is actually only one personally healthy reason to have an intimate relationship, besides the traditional propagation of the species (which doesn't take that long if that's all you want), and that is this:

The purpose of an intimate relationship is to enhance your development faster and/or better than if you were alone.

So, if your intimate relationships aren't helping you develop your potential then just what the heck are you doing?

In light of the above, pen a few thoughts, including commitments, about your intimate relationships with significant others and friends:

_____
_____

_____

_____

_____

_____

_____

_____

_____

_____

25

Relationships: Work

Just the term "work environment" is open to so many definitions that it is difficult to write a solitary document that applies to your specific situation UNLESS we realize that there are certain underlying issues that are universal. For example, Maslow's hierarchy of needs gives us a big clue: Most people's motivation in the work place is to continually fill their gas-tanks in order to satisfy their *physiological, safety, belongingness, love,* or *self-esteem needs.*

People give up huge chunks of their *time* (life) in order to come to work to get their deficiency needs met. There is a quiet desperation in them *at all times,* running like a subconscious current, for fear that those needs won't be met. People will manipulate, lie, cheat, steal, and even hurt you if they think you are between them and their getting those needs met. Count on it. [Don't get paranoid, get real!]

In terms of your own stress management this is extremely useful information! Taking this information and combining it with a little common sense, you come up with some powerful insight. For example, if a dog is starving you don't give it a bowl of water. Likewise, if it's thirsting to death, don't give it a milk bone, right? In other words:

 If you give people what they want your life will be much easier!

Not only will your life be easier, but you are also going to be very popular! People who apply this principle are so rare that you will stick out like Florida. What this asks of you is to be aware enough to deduce what it is that other people think they need. Here are some typical scripts running through people's heads in each of Maslow's categories:

Physiological Needs
I need some food.
I need something to drink.
I need this room to be colder/hotter.
I need money in order to get my bodily needs outside of here met.

Safety Needs
Is my job secure?
Am I going to get hurt by _____ ?
Am I going to get physically hurt by/on the job?
I need money in order to get my or my family's safety needs outside of here met.

Belongingness Needs
Am I in the "in group"?
Am I accepted for being who I am?
Do I feel like I belong or that I fit in here?
Do I feel [psychologically] *comfortable here?*
I need money in order to get my belonging needs outside of here met.

Love Needs
Does anyone care about me here?
Do they appreciate my unique attributes?
I need money in order to get my love needs outside of here met.

Self-Esteem Needs
Do my achievements count?
Will I get credit for what I do?
Am I going to advance here in terms of promo-tions, increased status, merit pay, bigger office, etc.?
I need money in order to get my self-esteem needs outside of here met.

[And just in case you work with rare individuals]

Self-Actualization Needs
Am I growing or being stifled here?
Am I being beneficially challenged here?
Am I being given the opportunities to express my real identity here?
I need money in order to get my self-actualization needs outside of here met.

So, the challenge is to train yourself to get more and more accurate at diagnosing "where people are coming from" and then be willing to meet their needs if and when you can.

This does not mean you should neglect **your** needs, not at all. Actually it directly increases your ability to meet your needs to think of others. If they are content, then they are not going to get in your way, right? When the dog is fed, it goes away to take a nap.

Satisfying Deficiency Needs is a Highway to Growth

Maslow also points out that by taking care of deficiency needs, you are eventually pulled up to the *self-actualization* category. For as long as you or they are hungry or thirsty or feel alienated, it will be difficult to think about, much less work towards, personal development. In effect, this information encourages us to take care of deficiency needs so that we **can** self-actualize!

Think of some co-workers and list what you think some of their needs that you can satisfy might be:

_____

_____

_____

_____

_____

_____

_____

_____

_____

_____

_____

_____

_____

_____

_____

_____

_____

_____

_____

_____

_____

_____

_____

_____

_____

_____

The Top 10 Stress Prevention Tips at Work

And here are a few other little rules that will smooth out potential stressors before they appear.

1. *Know your job.* The more competent, up to date, and clear about your job you are the more effective and guilt-free you will be. Learn.

2. *Don't procrastinate.* There is perhaps no better way to create stress than by putting things off.

3. *Confront.* If you have a disagreement, or a rumor is starting, get on top of it right away with the most powerful tool: *Truth.*

4. *Build relationships.* Healthy, supportive, productive relationships don't just happen, you have to take care of them like a garden with tending, fertilizing and weeding.

5. *Be respectful.* I didn't say "nice" because often nice is just sugar-coated manipulation. Being respectful is simply living the golden rule.

6. *Never triangulate.* Refrain from back-biting, gossip, or rumor-mongering. This is a very dumb, though prevalent, practice as it either comes back to haunt you socially, or it poisons your insides. You cannot win by talking about people behind their backs. Got something to say? Say it to their face, address it in writing to them, or zip your lip.

7. *Do at least 10% more than you are supposed to do.* Most people try to do 10%

less. By quietly doing 10% more than what your job description calls for **you will be noticed.** Part of the 10% philosophy is owning a clear conscience that you are doing your best and honestly earning your wages.

8. *Get to work 5 to 10 minutes early.* Getting to work early insures that you wont have that frenetic start that sets a bad tone for the rest of the day. Also, if you happen to have a traffic delay with a train or whatever, you have a built-in buffer.

9. *Drink more juice and water and less caffeine.* Being wired all day is rough on the nervous system and promotes jittery and paranoid thinking. Nothing wrong with a stiff coffee in the morning, but then go for healthier liquids the rest of the day. Instead of a coffee break, try a short walk, do CCB for 5 minutes, or take a 5-minute powernap.

10. *Relate your job to a personal mission.* If your job does not have a deeper sense of *meaning* for you, you will eventually be stressed by boredom, fatigue, frustration, etc., even if it is putting food on the table. Start looking around for more training, education, and/or other job opportunities if this one is meaningless to you.

26

Relationships: Parent-Child

One of the most stressful relationships in our lives is with our children. The major reason for this is because children's needs are naturally constant but constantly changing. Remember that our definition of a *stressor* is anything that asks us to make a change. So, although it may feel like kids are deliberately being a royal pain, it is just part of their nature to be a Pez dispenser of needs. This is why when we were teenagers our mothers told us to make sure we were "ready" to have kids. Of course, we all listened.

I take somewhat of a hard line on the need for quality relationships between parents and their children. I published a book titled *Resolving Unfinished Business* wherein I listed over 130 forms of abuse and neglect that happen to children and, *if they survive,* then continue to affect them as adults. It almost makes you nauseous to read that list. Parents abuse their children physically, emotionally, verbally, mentally, and spiritually, and almost always justify it or deny it, basically leaving the kid holding the bag.

I maintain that there are two major reasons that parents "lose it" with children: 1) the parent already has ineffective tools (either missing or inappropriate) to handle stress, then 2) the additional load of children's demands puts them "over the top" often resulting in incidences of abuse/ neglect.

So, my hope for this particular section of the book is to break this cycle by providing to you that are parents some information and tools that can replace that ineffectiveness and stop a vicious cycle.

Two Vicious Cycles

Actually there are two vicious cycles involved here. The first is intergenerational in that those of us who were treated badly by our parents under stress tend to repeat the same patterns with our children. Sometimes we do just the opposite which is equally ineffective. For example, if my Mom watched my every move, never let me make any choices, and basically suffocated me with "Smother Love" then: a) I might unconsciously duplicate her methods; or, b) I might reject her methods so much that when I have children I do the opposite and provide a distant hands-off strategy of parenting.

Now the child feels neglected, which is just another form of abuse (*neglect* is covert abuse). Yet, in my heart I really felt I was doing so well because I wasn't "being like my Mom" who I saw as a terrible model of parenting. So—the cycle continues—my son grows up and says to himself, "My Dad was never there for me and that was so painful, I am going to be a "good parent" and be involved in everything my kid does." In other words he turns out to be his grandmother (who of course is on the sidelines encouraging him to be just like her!). Get the picture?

180 degrees from nuts is still nuts.

The other vicious cycle is built into the inter-action with you and your child. This is simple to see (especially over at your neighbor's house!) if one just steps back a tad. When a child makes a demand of a parent and it is not properly per-ceived/received by the parent the child just "ups the volume" because the need still is not met. Now at this moment you would think some insight would dawn on the parent, e.g., "Wow, this strat-egy I tried with Timmy was ineffective—I must have missed the mark, so I will try another tactic." But, no, most parents just repeat the same strategy, only a notch louder such as, "I said NO!" Well, the need still is not met, and the child "asks" again in their own way, and will continue to in some form until the parent either gets it and responds appro-priately or, more usually, the parent gets so frus-trated that they abuse the child just to shut up a request that they feel they can't meet.

HAPPENS ALL THE TIME!
HAPPENS ALL THE TIME!
HAPPENS ALL THE TIME!
HAPPENS ALL THE TIME!

 If what you want is not what you need
no amount will ever be enough.

If what you "want" is for the child to be quiet but what you "need" is the ability to fulfill the child's needs, your requests for quiet will never be enough.

Children are not eloquent speakers! Wouldn't it blow your mind if a four year-old came up to you and said,

"Mother Dearest, I have been monitoring my deficiency needs rather closely today and I am beginning to notice that my sugar level is now dropping rapidly. If this continues I will get increasingly irritable and, since I am unable to articulate my needs clearly, probably begin to take it out on my sister by pinching her until she screams. Thus, do you think I might be able to have a bite or two of food in order to increase the amount of glucose in my bloodstream thus heading off unpleasantness all around?"

Parents are supposed to be smarter than their children—and certainly *wiser*—in that we have a broader perspective on what is occurring and can see possible future consequences resulting from present day behaviors. As designed by nature, children have their "noses up against the window of life," and the other half of the successful team is the mature adult who remembers what it was like to be a child, but also sees "the rest of the story" coming down the road and coaches the child along to be able to handle life effectively. Has anyone ever spoken more wisely of this than Kahlil Gibran in a section of *The Prophet*?

And a woman who held a babe against her bosom said,
Speak to us of Children.
And he said:
Your children are not your children.
They are the sons and daughters of Life's longing for itself.

They come through you but not from you,
And though they are with you yet they belong not
to you.

You may give them your love but not your
thoughts,
For they have their own thoughts.
You may house their bodies but not their souls,
For their souls dwell in the house of tomorrow,
which you cannot visit, not even in your dreams.
You may strive to be like them,
but seek not to make them like you.
For life goes not backward nor tarries with yester-
day.

You are the bows from which your children as liv-
ing arrows are sent forth.
The archer sees the mark upon the path of the infi-
nite, and He bends you with His might that His
arrows may go swift and far.
Let your bending in the archer's hand be for glad-
ness;
For even as He loves the arrow that flies,
so He loves also the bow that is stable.

I deliberately place Gibran's poem here as a message of truth and understanding such that your *perspective* is altered. Don't take this lightly as,

 Perspective is everything!

Perspective shapes our reality, and children serve as constant reminders of this. Instead of seeing your little ones as just "naïve semi-humans" who don't truly understand the world, try seeing

them as having a different perspective on life that can teach you something.

The Top 10 Things Children Can Teach Us

1. How to see things with fresh-eyes.
2. How to focus our attention.
3. How to be spontaneous.
4. How to be creative.
5. How to love without judgement.
6. How to stay in the moment.
7. How to rebound.
8. How to forgive quickly.
9. Enthusiasm for life!
10. How to eat only the center of a sandwich guilt-free. (Question conventionality.)

The bottom line is: Be smart enough to read between the lines to see your child's expressed needs, then address the needs, thus satisfying the child.

 Address the need behind the expression of it.

This is good parenting because it informs the child clearly:

1. They are in competent, intelligent hands, and
2. They are cared for, so
3. They can relax, and
4. Just be a kid.

This does a lot for **you** as well as for the child. Children need this kind of reassurance in order to handle their own stress with stability. You are the only buffer between them and a world that eats children, and they subconsciously know this. When you can reassure them that they are in competent hands then they won't be so *desperate*. I see a lot of kids that are flat-out desperate, clawing and cloying after their parents with a frantic hunger for comfort and encouragement—but often acting it out in very obnoxious ways. I don't blame the kids. I blame *ignorance*—ignorance of the sign language being sent and falling on deaf ears.

Top 10 Stress Prevention Tips for Children

1. They need lots of hugs and reassurance (more than you can imagine as reasonable).

2. They need to lovingly and firmly learn limits (how far they can go).

3. BUT set as few rules as possible—remember you don't want to wind up being a policeman instead of a parent!

4. They need to lovingly and firmly learn boundaries (how far they should let other people go with them) yet you have to balance that off with them learning safely from their own mistakes, too.

5. Send this message clearly to your children over and over: "I will let you run your life healthfully, but if you cannot or will not, I WILL! **You have a choice.**"

6. Children need to be encouraged by being told what they are doing "right" more than what they are doing "wrong" (research shows that in the total pool of positive vs. negative comments made to children by parents over 90% are negative).

7. Health, rest, and nutrition needs are a must-meet need (sending one of the deepest of messages: "I love you enough to preserve the quality of your life.")

8. Listen to what children mean not what they say or display.

9. Expand their horizons healthfully (under your guidance get them out there to experience the great things of life).

10. Teach them to clearly see the connections between what they think, what they do, and the outcomes in their lives. (Primary Domino Thinking)

By doing these ten things deliberately many of children's needs will be met and they will be a lot more serene and happy, definitely lowering the number of stressors coming in your direction from them. This also allows you to rest assured that you are doing the best you know how, which relieves that constant pressure/guilt created by doubt in parents.

Summary

I am going to summarize with a hard line again. If you object to the tips above, get over it. You are *responsible,* as this is the consequence of having a child. They didn't ask to be born, but now they need you and depend on you. Be a full-grown adult for them, and do the right thing. They aren't children forever, and you will have your life back sooner than you think. Create a legacy you are proud of! **You will never regret it!**

Some day you will watch your grandchildren being treated a certain way by your adult child— what will you want to see in that mirror?

Of course, a lot of other information in this book will work between parent and child. For example, I strongly suggest you teach your child how to do Conscious Connected Breathing. Kids love it and it gives them a tangible thing to do while pausing to reflect, as well as a way to relax. I have known of several parents who take breathing breaks with their children as one way of having some quality time together.

Learning the skill of *prioritizing* is another important thing to teach children so that they maximize their effectiveness and prevent unnecessary stressors from infiltrating their lives.

Learning about *metacognition,* or how to think about your thinking while your thinking, is an essential skill for children. Understanding *Primary Domino Thinking* is a great gift for a parent to hand to a child. (*Primary Domino Thinking for Children* will be out in the year 2000! Another fine book in the *PDT* Series!)

Journal some ideas that you are going to put into action with your child based on what you have read and learned (just ONE good idea can be worth a fortune in your relationship):

_____
_____
_____
_____
_____
_____
_____
_____
_____
_____
_____
_____
_____
_____
_____
_____
_____
_____
_____
_____

V

THE SECRET COMPARTMENT: SPIRITUALITY AND STRESS

27

The Secret Compartment

I call *spirituality* the "secret compartment" of effective stress management because it is so very personal and highly emotionally charged in nature. [Even as I write this I am wondering *how* to say to you what I am going to say—a sign to me that I am aware of its sensitive nature.]

Spirituality is even more personal and emotionally charged than one's sexuality. The high charge surrounding *spirituality* is because it is concerned with one's very essence and its relationship with that which is most real to us "outside" ourselves. It includes who we believe ourselves to be, our identity, our purpose, and our destiny. It's the BIG piece of information running the guidance system that determines our trajectory through this thing we call *life.*

As such, our *spirituality* provides an underlying blueprint for how we are going to respond to the stressors we meet as we travel our personal highway of life. If—and I mean IF—you are going to do anything at all about your automatic knee-jerk reflexive reactions to life's stressors then you must be willing to unearth and examine your spiritual belief system (or lack thereof) and how that sets you up for specific patterns of response. The good news is that the very act of clarifying this often murky arena starts straightening things out for us.

I cannot hold this discussion for you here on these pages. It is something you must be willing to do for yourself. But I can prime your pump!

The Two Schools of Spirituality

There are two distinctive schools of general spiritual thought that, at first glance, appear miles apart. They are closely related to the two ends of the continuum on Locus of Control issues in chapter 2.

The first is closely aligned with what I call the *little speck philosophy:* I am but a mere grain of sand on the cosmic beach and there is either nothing I can do that will make a difference anyway and/or a supreme being is pulling all the strings on my puppet existence, so why bother trying at all?

The second is: Either I am a separate entity in the universe and it is totally up to me to run the show called "my life"; or a religious take on this is that, yes, there is a supreme being but it is very remote after giving me all my tools/abilities/ potentialities and turning me loose on my own.

I want to make it clear that neither of these is ineffective unto itself. If something appears depressing about these it is not the belief system, but, rather, the way you regard them. [Just as *Happiness is an inside job,* so is depression an inside job. Neither happiness nor depression can be thrust upon you without your cooperation!]

28

Detachment as a Technique

Eastern philosophies recognized the pitfalls of stress centuries ago and have since preached that enlightenment consists of complete acceptance. There is the story of the enlightened Buddhist farmer whose only horse ran away. His neighbors tried to console him but he would only say: "That could be good. That could be bad." A few days later, his horse returned bringing back with it two more horses, tripling the farmer's wealth. The neighbors wished to celebrate his good fortune but he would only say: "That could be good. That could be bad." Then the farmer's son broke his leg trying to train one of the new wild horses: "That could be good. That could be bad." A few days later a band of roving mercenaries ravaged the countryside, conscripting all able-bodied young men for front-line mortal combat. The farmer's son, of course, was excluded thanks to his broken leg. Guess what the farmer said?

Classic Eastern philosophy proposes initial blanket acceptance of everything through complete detachment. It is the ultimate stress strategy, but it can be quite a stretch for some of us at first. Detachment doesn't always appeal to our Western minds. We often feel that this approach constitutes an infringement on the values, morals or even our personalities (not to mention our egos) which

209

accentuate determination and aggression if "you're going to get anywhere."

Detachment through initial total acceptance, however, is an option that's always available to us and no doubt we could all use it much more frequently and, in the process, spare ourselves mountains of stress and grief while teaching ourselves a thing or two about humility.

How to Detach

Here are several strategies, or roads, to detachment. They all have their different names and schools of origination, but I am going to cut to the chase a little and speak generically.

 You can't control everything

I mean who are you, Superman/woman? Are you going to deny yourself the privilege of just being a human being that is allowed to let destiny, fate, or other people have their say in what's going on?

 Have faith

As an active full-time psychotherapist I used to go to a Trappist monastery every 6-months to get my own head screwed back on straight. I had a dear friend there, Father Damien, who would very patiently listen to me unload my frustrations, fears, etc. One particular weekend evening as we went for a stroll out through the Kentucky farmlands just before sunset, I was venting a lot of self-doubts and anxiety about my ability to make sure that I always did just the right thing for my clients. I was really on a roll, just verbally hand-wringing every word as we walked, my head down. Father Damien suddenly stopped walking and interrupted me in mid-sentence. He reached over and smoothed my brow with his soft warm hands, looked lovingly into my eyes and said, "Tony, you worry too much. Someone 2000 years ago took this all on so you wouldn't have to. You don't have to worry about a thing. Your job is just to sit back and enjoy the ride." I wept, because I knew instantly that he was right. Why was I shouldering a world that had already been saved? Sometimes we just forget.

 Respect others

Trying to run other people's lives is disrespectful. You can't possibly know what they need to go through in this life to learn what they need to learn. Secondly, when you decide for others you are really saying to them, "You poor, pathetic being, I know you can't handle your own life. You must be s-o-o-o grateful that I am here to do it for you!" Think on this one. Don't you have enough to do running *your* life?

 It just doesn't matter

That great American philosopher, Bill Murray, said it so well in the movie, *Meatballs*. His camp team was preparing to play another camp's team in a sporting event that was obviously going to end in certain disaster. In a meeting the night before the game, the whole camp was glumly contemplating their upcoming humiliation the next day. When despondency and self-pity reach an all time high in the group Bill Murray begins pounding on the floor with his hand and chanting over and over, "It just doesn't matter!" At first, everyone is shocked, then annoyed with him, but he doesn't let up until one, then two, then everyone joins him and they are all pounding, yelling and laughing, "It just doesn't matter!"

And, of course, usually it doesn't! In 5 years who will care? Maybe even tomorrow?

 It all works out despite you not because of you

I bet you have proof of this one, don't you? [See *Have Faith*]

 Do your best and leave the rest

If you feel you have given it your best shot then let it go. You are almost *never* in charge of outcomes. I can schedule the picnic, send out the invitations, order the buns, pick up the soda pop, get the recreation equipment, etc., but after that it just isn't up to me to make sure everyone has a good time: *That's up to them.*

I also don't control the weather—that's up to someone/something else, too!

After doing all I can legitimately do to fulfill my responsibility to commitments I have made, I should be busy just making sure *I* have a good time!

You gotta love it!

No matter what happens, you might as well say "*YES!*" to it. It sits a lot easier in your gut, and you actually haven't given up the right to change it either. As a matter of fact, it is a lot easier to change something when you love it than it is when you resist it.

And, gosh, are you a LOT more fun to be around!

 How important is it?

Perspective. What an important concept! I guarantee that the people who committed suicide on Wall Street during the Great American Depression had no spiritually detached perspective on the matter of the importance of money in their lives. Talk about over-magnifying the importance of something! But sometimes people get just as excited about the garage door being left open, or a child bringing home a B in a course they formerly received an A in. You'd think the world was coming to an end, Chicken Little!

It is difficult to appreciate a painting with your nose pressed against it.

Once you have found your spiritual niche, events in your life take on a new perspective because they are measured against a different standard providing a new surety in making decisions about how to regard things—what is *truly* important, and what is not. Needless to say, it is easier to *detach* from things if they have consciously been ruled unimportant.

What if I haven't found my spiritual niche?

If you often feel empty, meaningless, lost, or like you have a big hole in your chest, it is a sign that you have not found your spiritual niche **yet.** This is often confused with *depression* (which it is *not!*) by even counselors and psychiatrists. More often it is simply a sign that it is time for you to go on your own Vision Quest.

29

The Personal Vision Quest

Vision Quests are performed by some in the Native American tradition of going off alone into nature with a minimum supply of food and bedding to contemplate one's purpose in life. Some do it at a monastery, in a motel, or in a seminar. It doesn't matter *how* you do it, it just matters that you *do it.*

If you are limited in time or resources right now, but still want to get started, here is a convenient technique to do a modern day Vision Quest.

Block out a couple of hours (at least) to begin with and go to a large bookstore and/or modern library. Go there alone with the attitude that you are seeking answers for the meaning and direction of your life. You do this by just wandering the aisles and gravitating to the sections that appeal to you and simply begin reading what interests or "draws" you.

If you have no idea where to start, I usually suggest starting with the self-help section, but also include metaphysics, religion, philosophy, and recovery sections as well. Avoid prejudging like the plague. Try to remember just how important the task is and resist hurrying, chit-chat, or being distracted into the arts & crafts, sporting, fiction, etc., sections.

You may need to do this in several time seg-
ments at different stores, libraries, or reading
rooms, moving from one topic to another as you
are led. Don't hurry; this is too important.

Relationship of the Mission and Vision Statements

At some point an interplay with the Mission
Statement exercise on page 156 can help as well.
Remember that a Vision Statement is *spiritual* in
nature and is concerned with discovering **why** you
exist. A Mission Statement is more applied, and is
concerned with **what** and **how** you are going to
live your vision on a daily basis. The statements
are separate and involve two different processes to
derive them. They do feed off one another, and you
can develop them in tandem quite nicely if that fits
your style.

Write Your Personal Vision Statement

Although they take some digging to uncover,
and they are a core-important theme of your life,
Vision Statements are usually quite short and
extremely poignant. Write your Vision Statement
when you feel it right to do so: *I am here to . . .*

_____
_____
_____
_____
_____
_____
_____
_____

Sample Vision Statements:

Dalai Lama: "To be kind to every person I meet."

Marian College: "To be the best liberal arts college in the world."

Your personal coach: "To teach meaningful and liberating knowledge and to have a good time doing it!"

Now that you have developed a Vision **and** a Mission Statement, you should have some fairly good insights on where your stress-control issues are coming from, right? Write down some changes you are going to make as a result of this experience:

_____

_____

_____

_____

_____

_____

_____

_____

_____

_____

_____

_____

_____

_____

_____

_____

_____

_____

_____

_____

_____

30

Conclusion

We are **not** at the mercy of our minds. We are **not** at the mercy of our bodies. We are **not** at the mercy of our emotions. And we are not at the mercy of our social relationships.

a) Intellectually, we have choices available to us. We have the freedom to choose how much credence or weight to give various ideas or beliefs that pop into our heads. In addition, there are a variety of tools available to improve our minds and the quality of our thoughts, such as broadening our minds through reading, conversation and humor, or focusing our minds through reflection, meditation, affirmations, visualization or self-hypnosis, etc., etc.

b) When distress manifests itself physically as illness, injury, pain, etc., we are not helpless. We have many healing options to deal with it directly at that level: taking prescriptions, getting more rest and relaxation, improving our lifestyle (diet, exercise), getting body work (chiropractic, physical therapy, massage) and so on.

c) Emotionally, we have options as well. Although our culture, like many others, is sadly deficient in psychological methods to handle emotions, moods and feelings, skills and tools can be developed such as

Conscious Connected Breathing, Vivation, Primary Domino Thinking, meditation, Neurolinguistic Programming (N.L.P.), hypnosis, etc.

d) Socially, whether with friends, lovers, colleagues, or our children, we are *partners* in those relationships and therefore, have *influence.* We have choices to utilize that influence to *upgrade* those relationships such that they serve all participants including ourselves. Some of our influence can be expressed through establishing our mission in life, then prioritizing, examining our expectations, obeying the six sacred sacraments, communicating clearly, and being aware of the importance of satisfying needs.

e) Spiritually, we need to get clear with ourselves what our vision in life is, and then learn how to detach from results of our best-laid plans.

Crossover Effects

It is important to realize that stress on one level may often be dealt with best by applying techniques on another level. For example, many people find that vigorous exercise wards off depression or lethargy. Professional athletes have demonstrated that visualization or mental focusing can be emotionally relaxing **and** improve physical performance. Norman Cousins cured his fatal disease through humor and laughter. We have also discovered that clearing up emotional stress does wonders for both our bodies and our minds.

The bottom line is that any stress reduction or stress management program should be holistic.

Any serious approach should include tools and activities on all levels: mental, emotional, physical, social and spiritual.

Dynamic stress-busters realize that an effective program involves willingness to look at one's *trajectory* in life, which is why it is so very important to have a personal vision of why one is on this planet and a sense of mission about carrying that out. This is then followed by persistent and consistent healthy choices in ways of thinking, feeling and acting.

And never forget the true objective of healthy stress management:

 Have even more fun!

A Note from Your Coach

If you have read and applied all the way through the book, HOORAY for you! Now, I ask you to do two things:

1. **Commit** to using at least one tool from this book *on a daily basis*. Then, **consciously commit** to perfecting the ones most applicable to your life until they become second nature. That means **please keep the book around and use it!**

2. **Remember** that this book is mostly about *life management*—**your** life! *The Essential Guide* provides a plethora of ways to stay in control of that precious possession and get more out of it than perhaps you ever dreamed. Live every day as if it is your last; pretend that every person you meet is

doing their last day, too. In this way (once you get over the frantic part and detach a little!) you will realize how important it is to live a quality life and stay in charge of it to keep it that way.

Thank you for your dedication to taking care of yourself. It is the greatest gift you have to give to yourself and all of us, especially your family.

A note to you that have not read the whole book: Do so now if you can; if not, keep the book around and read a few pages here and there until you are swept away with the wisdom of dedicating yourself to living in the direction of a stress-free life! Why? Because the alternative reeks!

Make a great life, day by day.

Anthony S. Dallmann-Jones, Ph.D.
Fond du Lac, Wisconsin

APPENDICES

I

Dallmann-Jones
Stress Test

In the past 12 months, which of these has happened to you?

If a stressor has occurred more than once, multiply before placing the total in the slot. Then add up the total and read below.

Event

Death of a spouse	99	_____
Death of a child	98	_____
Disabled child	97	_____
Single parenting	96	_____
Divorce	91	_____
Remarriage	89	_____
Depression	89	_____
Abortion	89	_____
Child's Illness	87	_____
Infertility	87	_____
Marriage	85	_____
Spouse illness	85	_____
Death of close family member	84	_____
Crime victimization	84	_____
Fired at work	83	_____
Husband's retirement	82	_____
Parenting parents	81	_____
Raising teens	80	_____
Chemical dependency	80	_____

Parents illness	78	_____
Pregnancy	78	_____
Marital separation	78	_____
Singlehood	77	_____
Moving	76	_____
Adoption	74	_____
Jail term	72	_____
Personal injury/illness	68	_____
Death of close friend	68	_____
Retirement	68	_____
Adult son/daughter moving back in	61	_____
Change of financial status	61	_____
Spouse begins or stops work	58	_____
Personal retirement	58	_____
Marital reconciliation	57	_____
Commuting	57	_____
Christmas/Holy Days	56	_____
Change in health of family member	56	_____
Foreclosure of mortgage/loan	55	_____
Sex difficulties	53	_____
Addition of family member	51	_____
Change to different line of work	51	_____
Business readjustment	50	_____
Mortgage over $20,000	48	_____
Change of residence	47	_____
Change (+ or –) in number of arguments with spouse	46	_____
Change in responsibilities at work	46	_____
Begin school term	45	_____
End school term	45	_____
Trouble with boss	45	_____
Revision of personal habits	44	_____
Trouble with in-laws	43	_____
Vacation	43	_____
Change in living conditions	42	_____
Son or daughter leaving home	41	_____
Outstanding personal achievement	38	_____

Change in work hours or conditions	36	_____
Change in school	36	_____
Minor violations of law	30	_____
Change in eating habits	29	_____
Mortgage/loan under $20,000	27	_____
Change in sleeping habits	27	_____
Change in recreation	26	_____
Change in number of family get-togethers	15	_____
TOTAL		_____

This test is meant to illustrate the connection between "too much stress" (unresolved stressors) and physical illness. According to the two doctors, Holmes and Rahe, who created the first stress test along this line, if your score is under 150 stress units, you have only a 37% chance (or less) of getting sick within the next two years. If your score is between 150 and 300, the probability rises to 51%. And if your score is over 300, the odds are 4 to 5 (80%) that you will be sick during the next two years.

You don't like the message you have received here? You want to do something about it? Consider reducing the number of changes in your life. Stop setting yourself up for stress.

II

101
STRESS RELIEVERS

Things You Can Do or Start Today to Relieve, Eliminate, or Better Manage Stress in Your Life

1. Build select periods of refuge into your schedule. (It's called a 'vacation'—remember?)

2. Learn how to take breaks during the day.

3. Live within your budget—pay your bills.

4. Anything that you can control in your lifestyle, do so. (disorganization = maximum stressors!)

5. Keep your number of role responsibilities in line. ("*No!*" is the word, if you have forgotten.)

6. Be ready to streamline your schedule.

7. If possible avoid people who stress you.

8. Plan—avoid overextending yourself.

9. Learn to compromise. (Cooperation = Growth; Competition = Stress).

10. Accept what you cannot change (including other people).

11. Frequently ask yourself, "How do I feel?" and listen to the answer!

12. Nurture relationships worth developing (Fertilize friendships!)

13. Try a new perspective, i.e., flexibility.

14. Ask for feedback from a reliable source.

15. Always be prepared to wait.

16. Leave time for delays in traveling and appointments.

17. Develop TO-DO lists that are accomplishable—only write down what you will complete in one day!

18. Explore your spirituality in some way.

19. Breathe consciously and connectedly for 5 minutes or more.

20. Do something creative.

21. Go to an aquarium.

22. Start an aquarium.

23. Write a poem about your feelings.

24. Forgive someone you thought you never would.

25. Make peace with your parents (whether alive or dead).

26. Make peace with your children.

27. Relax, learn to relax, practice relaxing, relax about not relaxing.

28. Do yoga.

29. Get massaged.

30. Get Rolfed.

31. See a chiropractor.

32. Practice a martial art.

33. Practice a marital art.

34. Run, jog, walk—Move!
35. Go swimming.
36. Improve your diet.
37. Improve your wardrobe.
38. Improve your image and self-image.
39. Learn to love your job/work/career.
40. Improve your relationship with your boss.
41. Spend money.
42. Save money—start a new account.
43. Earn money.
44. Give away money.
45. Keep a journal of your feelings.
46. Enjoy your successes. (Roll around in 'em like a hound dog!).
47. Learn from, and let go of, your failures.
48. Read books.
49. Sit in a sauna.
50. Sit in a whirlpool.
51. Shower with a friend.
52. Sun bathe.
53. Sit in total silence while staying alert.
54. Go on a hike, explore.
55. Go camping.
56. Tell the whole truth as fast as possible.
57. Communicate better and more often with your loved ones.
58. Write yourself a letter.
59. Make some positive long-range goals.
60. Visualize success.
61. Do guided imagery of peaceful scenes.
62. Take a weekend trip.

63. Meditate.
64. See a movie.
65. Do some stretching exercises.
66. Learn to do affirmations.
67. Learn and apply self-hypnosis.
68. Make peace with your childhood.
69. Resolve destructive dualisms.
70. Get the right amount of sleep.
71. Make peace with money.
72. Invent something.
73. Learn to delegate.
74. Listen to easy music with headphones.
75. Get in touch with your body.
76. Make peace with death.
77. Make peace with God.
78. Make a retreat.
79. Try to enjoy everything for five minutes at a time.
80. Contact a long, lost friend.
81. Play with a pet.
82. Remember that a clock is a tool, not an enemy.
83. Learn Vivation (see Jim Leonard in Bib.)
84. Clean up and get organized.
85. Treat yourself to maid service.
86. Go out to a good restaurant.
87. Go to the beach, the mountains, the lake.
89. Uncover your healthy self-esteem.
90. Skip a meal.
91. Go on a fast.
92. Eat your dessert first.

93. Resurrect an old hobby.
94. Buy yourself a present.
95. Smile.
96. Tell a joke.
97. Travel.
98. Go to bed two hours earlier than usual once a week.
99. Take a wellness day off.
100. Eat a bowl of cereal; hold the spoon with your fist.
101. Pray.

III

20+ Stress Multipliers

How to Die Young

1. Stay in a job you hate.
2. Don't tell your significant other anything.
3. Avoid physical activity and sunshine.
4. Postpone all vacations.
5. Stuff all your feelings and emotions.
6. Try to be perfect.
7. Eat all the wrong foods.
8. Skimp on rest and sleep.
9. Never do anything silly, frivolous or fun.
10. Take yourself and life more seriously than necessary.
11. Dwell on all the world's political, social and economic problems (get obsessed with the evening news) and wallow in your helplessness to change any of it.
12. Convince yourself that you'll never have enough money.
13. Spend as much time as possible at work and as little as possible in leisure activities.
14. Try to do (be) several things at once.
15. Breathe shallowly and hold your breath.

16. Never try anything new.
17. Ignore your spiritual development and needs.
18. Hang around depressing, annoying and negative people.
19. Stay on bad terms with your parents and/or children.
20. Stop reading anything interesting.
21. If something bothers you, don't speak up.
22. Never play.
23. Add **your** favorite ways to burn yourself out:

_____

_____

_____

_____

_____

_____

_____

_____

_____

_____

_____

_____

_____

_____

_____

_____

_____

_____

_____

_____

_____

_____

Bibliography and Suggested Readings

Allen, James. *As A Man Thinketh.* Stamford, CT. Longmeadow Press, 1993.

Bach, Richard. *Jonathan Livingston Seagull.* New York: Avon Books, 1970.

Bennett, Hal Zina & Sparrow, Susan. *Follow Your Bliss.* New York: Avon Books, 1990.

Bry, Adelaide. *Visualizations: Directing the Movies Of Your Mind.* New York: Harper & Row, 1979.

Childre, Doc Lew. *Self Empowerment: The Heart Approach to Stress Management.* Boulder Creek, CA: Planetery Publications, 1992.

Chopra, Deepak. *Unconditional Life: Discovering the Power to Fulfill Your Dreams.* New York: Bantam, 1992.

_____. [Anything written by Deepak is golden.]

Cousins, Norman. *Head First . . . The Biology of Hope.* New York: P. Dutton, 1989.

Csikszentmihalyi, Mihaly. *FLOW: The Psychology of Optimal Experience.* New York: Harper & Row, 1990.

Dacher, Elliott. *PNI: The New Mind/Body Healing Program.* New York: Paragon House, 1993.

Dallmann-Jones, A.S. *PHOENIX FLIGHT MAN- UAL—Rising Above the Ashes of Ordinary*

Existence. Fond du Lac, WI: Three Blue Herons Pub., Inc., 1995.

Dallmann-Jones, A.S. *PRIMARY DOMINO THINKING—Creating The Life You Want.* Fond du Lac, WI: Wolf Creek Press, 1997.

Dallmann-Jones, A.S. *Resolving Unfinished Business.* Fond du Lac, WI: Three Blue Herons Pub., Inc., 1995.

Dienstfrey, Harris. *Where the Mind Meets the Body.* New York: HarperCollins, 1991.

Ellis, Albert & Harper, Robert. *A Guide To Rational Living.* No. Hollywood, CA: Wilshire Book Co., 1973.

Epstein, Gerald. *Healing Visualizations: Creating Health Through Imagery.* New York: Bantam, 1989.

Ferguson, Marilyn. *PragMagic.* New York: Pocket Books, 1990.

Fezler, William. *Imagery for Healing, Knowledge, and Power.* New York: Simon & Schuster, 1990.

Gawain, Shakti. *Creative Visualization.* New York: Bantam Books, 1985.

_____. T*he Path of Transformation.* Mill Valley, CA: Nataraj Pub., 1993.

Gibran, Kahlil. *The Prophet.* New York: Alfred A. Knopf, 1986.

Goleman, Daniel, and Joel Gurin (Editors) *Mind Body Medicine.* Yonkers, NY: Consumer Reports Books, 1993.

Hay, Louise. *The Power Is Within You.* Carson, CA: Hay House, Inc.,1991.

Helmstetter, Shad. *Choices.* New York: Pocket Books, 1989.

Helmstetter, Shad. *What To Say When You Talk To Yourself.* New York: Pocket Books, 1982.

Hendricks, Gay. *Conscious Breathing.* New York: Bantam Books, 1995.

Leonard, Jim. *The Skill of Happiness—Creating Daily Ecstasy With VIVATION.* Fond du Lac, WI: Three Blue Herons Publishing, Inc., 1996.

Leonard, Jim. *Your Fondest Dream.* Cincinnati: AVP Publishing, 1989.

Leonard, Jim & Laut, Phil. *Vivation: The Science of Enjoying All of Your Life.* Cincinnati: AVP Publishing, 1991.

Maslow, Abraham. *Motivation and Personality.* NY: Harpercollins College Division, 1987.

Palmer, Harry. *Living Deliberately.* Altamonte Springs, FL: Stars Edge International, 1994.

Palmer, Harry. *ReSurfacing.* Altamonte Springs, FL: Stars Edge International, 1994.

Paulus, Trina. *Hope for the Flowers.* New York: Paulist Press, 1972.

Peale, Norman Vincent. *You Can If You Think You Can.* Carmel, NY: Guideposts Assoc., Inc. 1974.

Sky, Michael. *Breathing: Expanding Your Power & Energy.* Santa Fe: Bear & Co. Publishing, 1990.

Tae Yun Kim. *Seven Steps To Inner Power.* San Rafael, CA: New World Library, 1991.

Wilde, Stuart. *Affirmations.* Taos, NM: White Dove, 1987.

_____. [Anything else written by Stuart, ever.]

You are encouraged to participate in Dr. Dallmann-Jones' live *Primary Domino Thinking* Seminars offered in locations around the globe. Please write for information on sponsoring a workshop or contracting with Dr. D-J as a speaker for your organization.

Institute for Transformational Studies
P.O. Box 1181
Fond du Lac, Wisconsin 54936-1181

Mission Statement: *The Institute exists to research, develop and produce vehicles, bridges and scaffoldings that transform knowledge into productive intelligence for the betterment of humankind.*

To this end, empowering and rejuvenating workshops, seminars, in-services, trainings, videotapes, and audio-tapes are available.

Inquire into personal coaching with Dr. D-J privately at Wolf Creek or by telephone.
Call 920-921-6991 between 9 a.m. and 5 p.m. CST to make arrangements.

The PRIMARY DOMINO THINKING Series

Specific topics for the series are derived from the mother book,

PRIMARY DOMINO THINKING
—Creating the Life You Want—
by Anthony S. Dallmann-Jones, Ph.D.
published in 1997 by Wolf Creek Press

Future books in the *PDT Series* are optimistically scheduled for publication as follows:

* August, 1998

    The PRIMARY DOMINO THINKING
    Daily Reader

* April, 1998

    The PRIMARY DOMINO THINKING
    Non-Diet Method to Weight Loss

* August, 1999

    ON PURPOSE
    —Discovering Your Life's Mission—
    (And Making It Happen)

* August, 2000

    ARO: Achieving Relative Obscurity
    in the New Millenium

* August, 2000

    PRIMARY DOMINO THINKING for Children

Books and Tapes by
Anthony S. Dallmann-Jones, Ph.D.

Primary Domino Thinking—
Creating the Life You Want
(The Mother Book of the PDT Series!)

Phoenix Flight Manual—
Rising Above the Ashes of Ordinary Existence
(Includes the conceptual framework, history,
case studies, and knowledge base of *Primary*
Domino Thinking.)

Resolving Unfinished Business—
Assessing the Effects of Being Raised
in a Dysfunctional Environment
(How your family of origin affects you today.)

The Expert Educator—
A Reference Manual of Teaching Strategies
for Quality Education
(A teaching methodology manual for
teachers of any content at any level.)

Primary Domino Thinking
The Video
(Learn this New Millennium Science from
Dr. Dallmann-Jones himself in 30 minutes!)

WOLF CREEK PRESS
P.O. Box 1181
Fond du Lac, WI 54937 USA

Order Form

Name _____

Address _____

City&State_____Zip _____

Tel_____Fax _____

E-dress: _____

__*Essential Guide to Stress Free Living*	$14.95=	_____
__*Primary Domino Thinking*	$12.95=	_____
__*PDT*—Video (30 min.color)	$29.95=	_____
__*Phoenix Flight Manual*	$14.95=	_____
__*Resolving Unfinished Business*	$12.95=	_____
__*The Expert Educator*	$19.95=	_____
__Primary Domino Keychain	$10.00=	_____

(Pewter, full-size #1 domino. Nice!)

(Wisc. Residents add 5% sales tax)   _____

S/H: $5 for the first item and $1 for
each additional item: _____

                                TOTAL:_____

Visa/MC #:_____

Exp. Date:_____

You may fax your order via our secured line: 920-921-7691
You may e-mail your order to: asdjones@iosys.net
Or mail to:
Wolf Creek Press
PO Box 1181
Fond du Lac, WI 54936-1181

Stores and wholesalers call: Associated Publishers Group
1-800-327-5113